Niagara-on-the-Lake Ontario Book 2 in Colour Photos, Saving Our History One Photo at a Time

Photography
by Barbara Raué
2015

Series Name:
Cruising Ontario

Book 103: Niagara-on-the-Lake Book 2

Cover photo: Victoria Street, Marrakech Mansion – see Page 32

Series Name: Cruising Ontario
Saving Our History One Photo at a Time
in colour photos

Other Books by Barbara Raué

Coins of Gold

Arrows, Indians and Love

The Life and Times of Barbara
Volume 1: Inventions That Have Enhanced My Life
Volume 2: Entertainment That I Have Enjoyed
Volume 3: East Coast Trips
Volume 4: Olympics Have Always Intrigued Me
Volume 5: Wonders of the World
Volume 6: Caribbean Cruises We Have Enjoyed
Volume 7: Animals
Volume 8: Storms and Other Major Disasters in My Lifetime
Volume 9: Wars, Terrorist Attacks and Major Disasters

The Cromwell Family Book

Laura Secord Discovered

Daddy Where Are You?

Visit Barbara's website to view all of her books
http://barbararaue.ca

The first permanent settlers of Niagara-on-the-lake were Butlers Rangers and other Loyalist refugees who arrived in 1778 when they began crossing from Fort Niagara to settle the west bank of the Niagara River. A town was laid out in a grid pattern of four-acre blocks and grew quickly, gaining prominence as the first capital of Upper Canada from 1792 to 1796. The town was captured by American forces on May 27, 1813; upon their withdrawal on December 13, 1813, the American forces burned the town.

Following Niagara's destruction, the citizens rebuilt mainly in the British classical architectural tradition, creating a group of structures closely related in design, material and scale. Spared from redevelopment, the town's colonial buildings eventually became one of its greatest resources. Beginning in the 1950s, residents rehabilitated and restored old structures, demonstrating an exceptional commitment to the preservation of local heritage.

The Niagara Agricultural Society (1792-1805) was devoted to the improvement of agriculture. Its members were mostly merchants, politicians, clergymen, and gentlemen farmers who met regularly for dinner and discussion. They introduced new varieties of fruit trees to the Niagara peninsula in 1794 and sponsored the province's first agricultural fair in Queenston in 1799. Although the society was short-lived, its scientific approach to farming anticipated the work of regional agricultural societies run by farmers after 1820.

Table of Contents

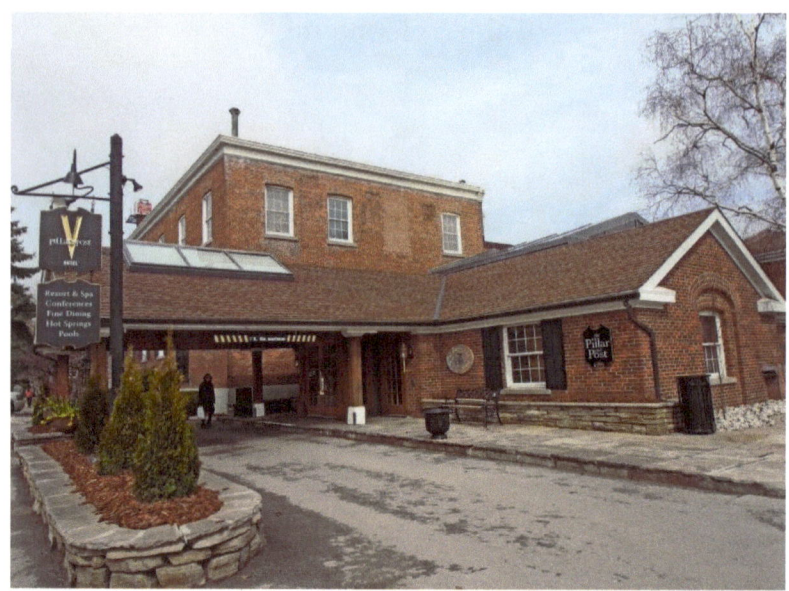

Pillar and Post's original structure was built in the late 1890s as a canning factory, and has been lovingly transformed into a fine hotel. You can still see its original purpose in the clean lines of the brick walls and in the impressive post-and-beam construction.

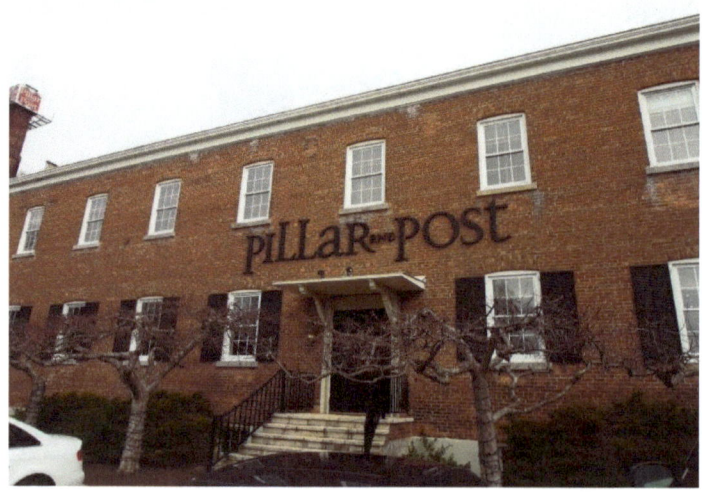

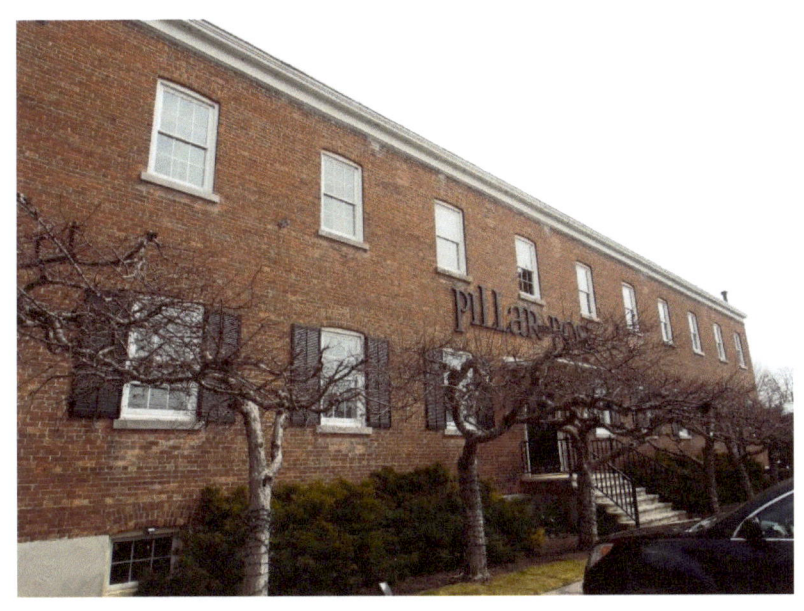

48 John Street - Pillar and Post

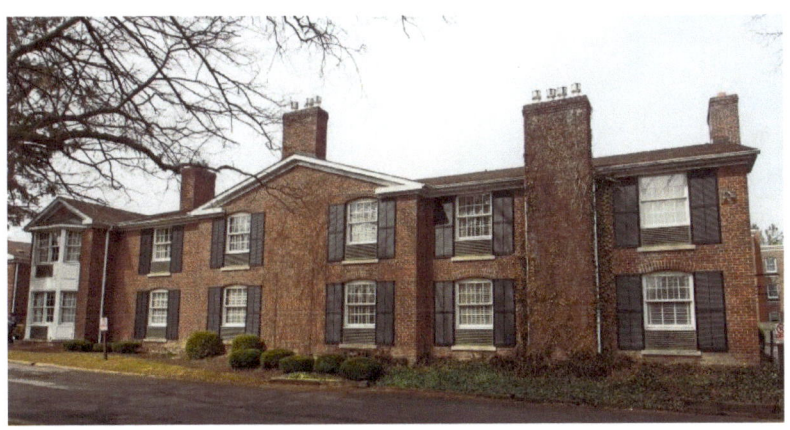

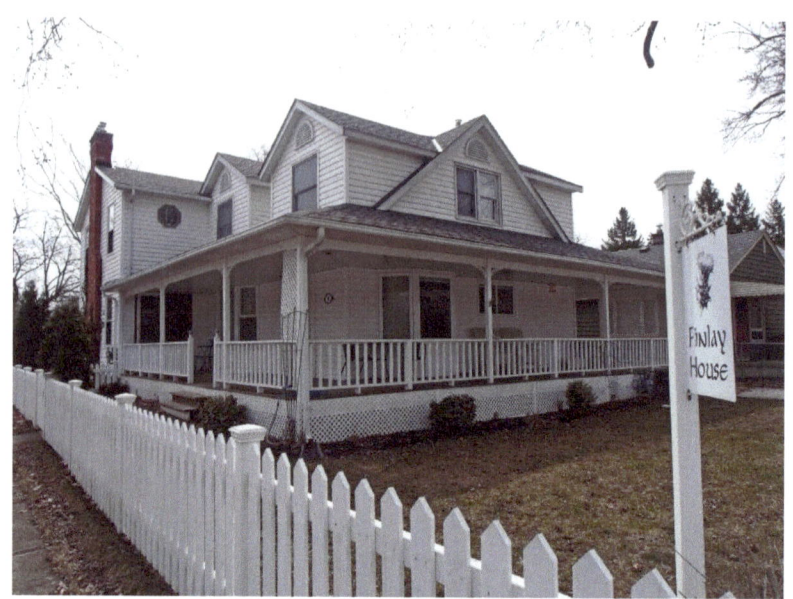

8 Nelles Street – Finlay House Bed and Breakfast

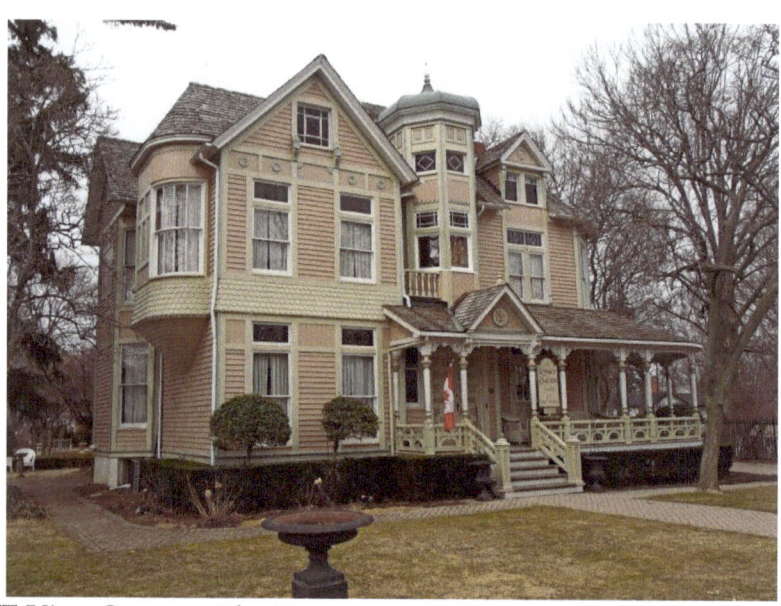

177 King Street – The Romance Collection Gallery featuring
the exclusive works of Trisha Romance and Tanya Jean
Peterson – Queen Anne style home

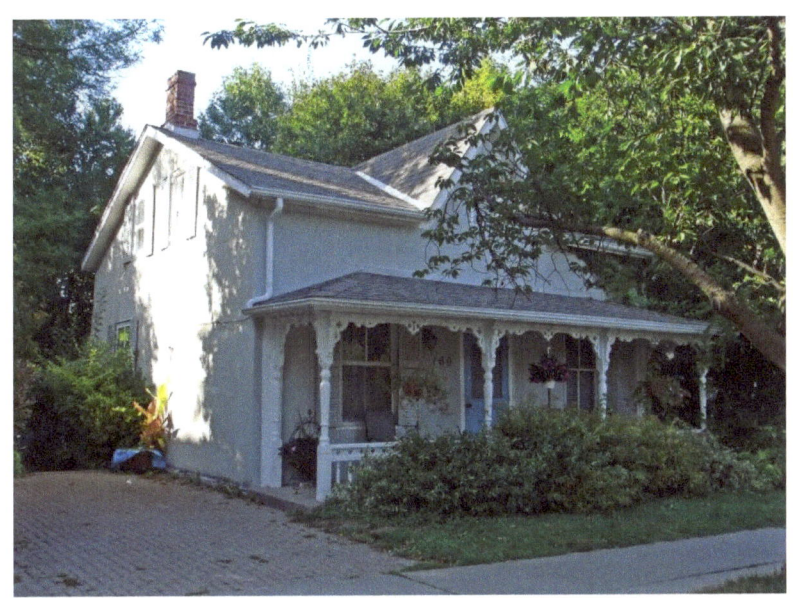

169 King Street – Gothic Revival

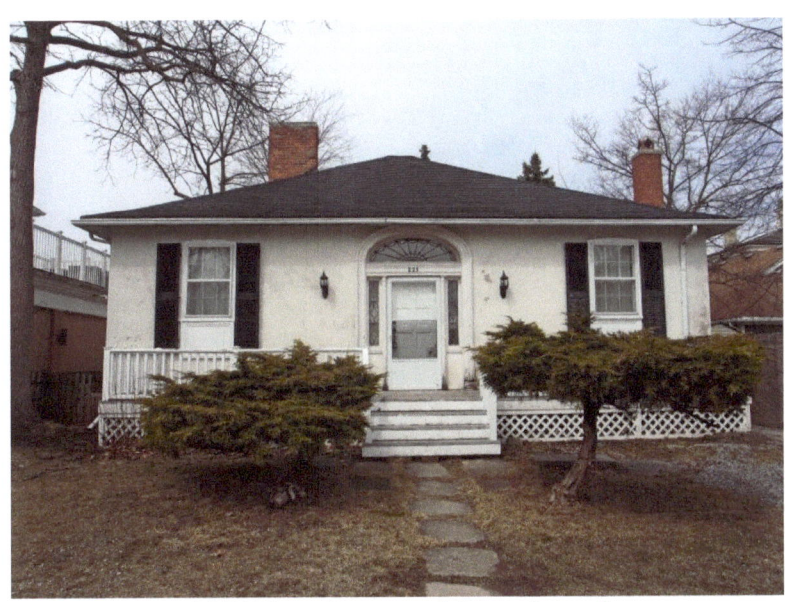

225 King Street – hipped roof

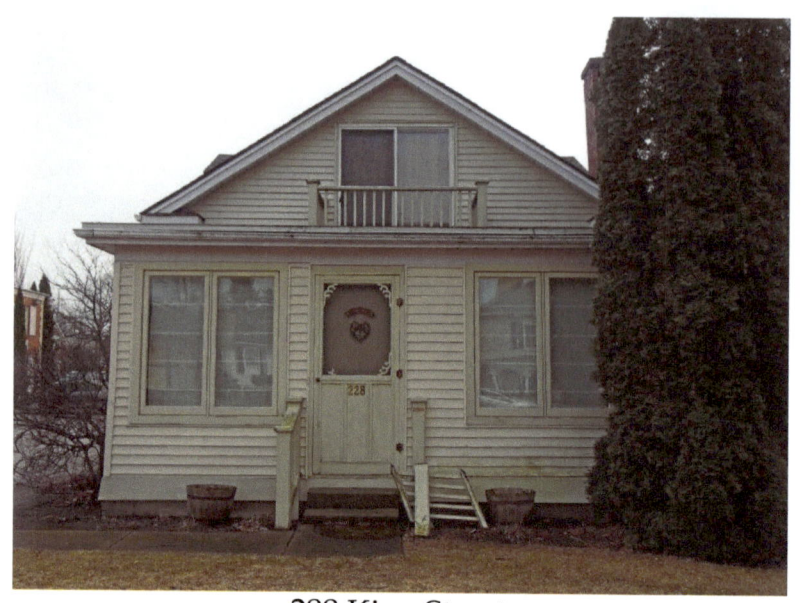

288 King Street

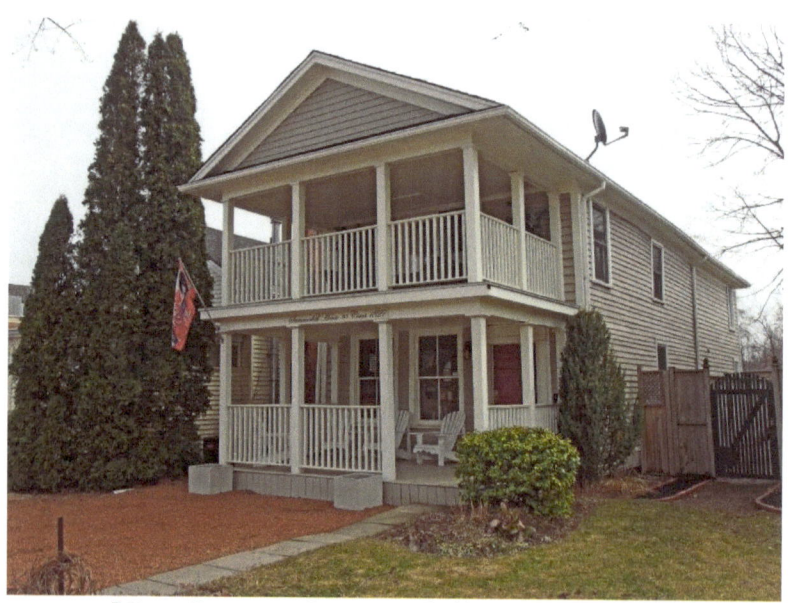

King Street – Summerhill House c. 1827

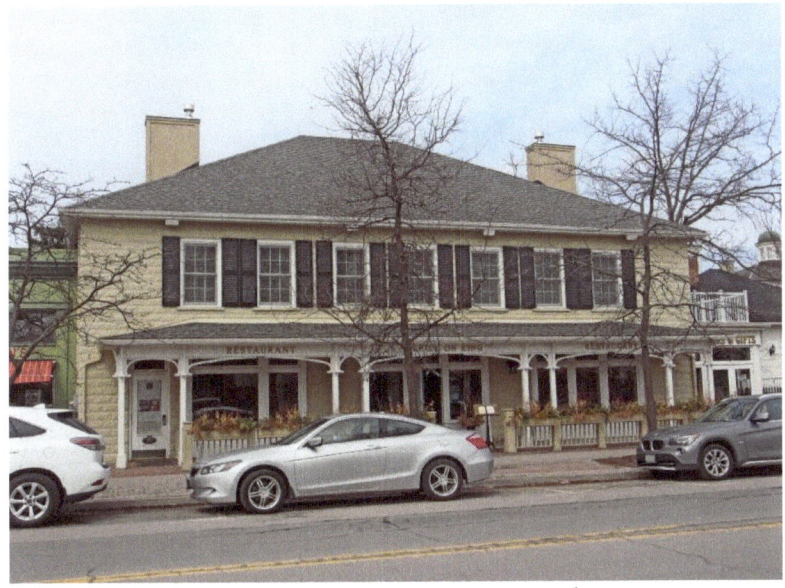

King Street – Georgian style

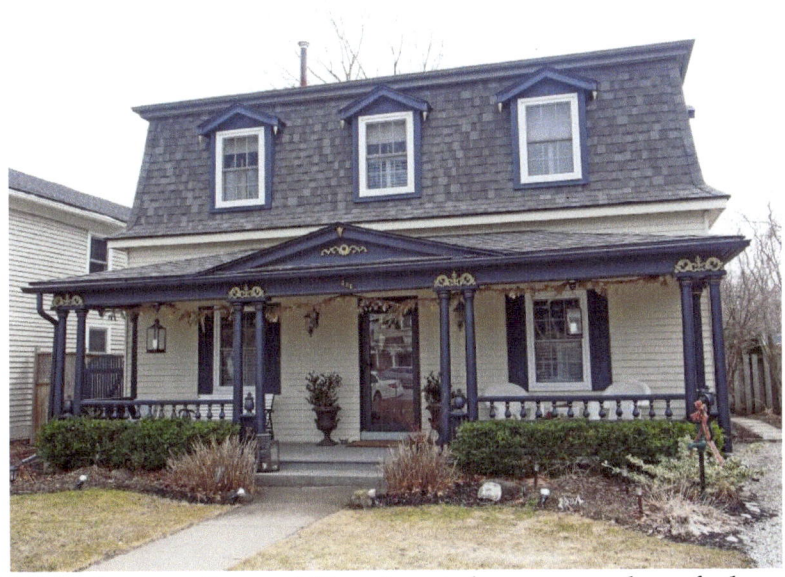

236 King Street – Second Empire style, mansard roof, dormers

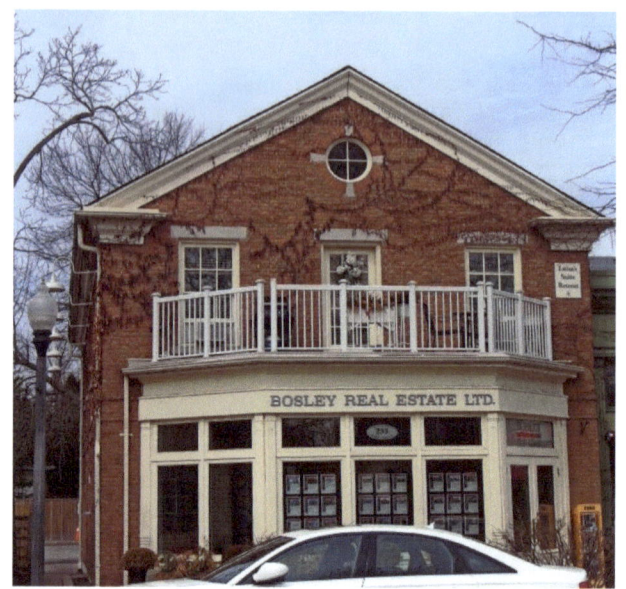

233 King Street

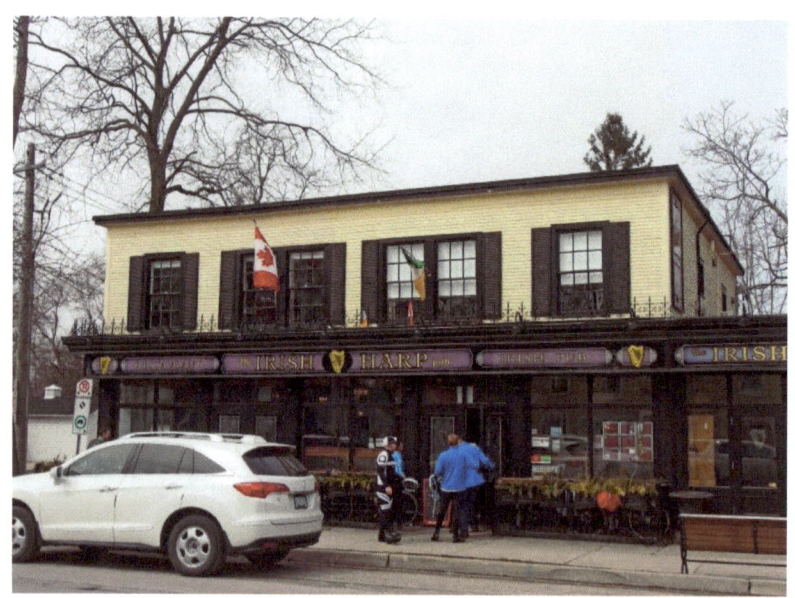

The Irish Harp Pub

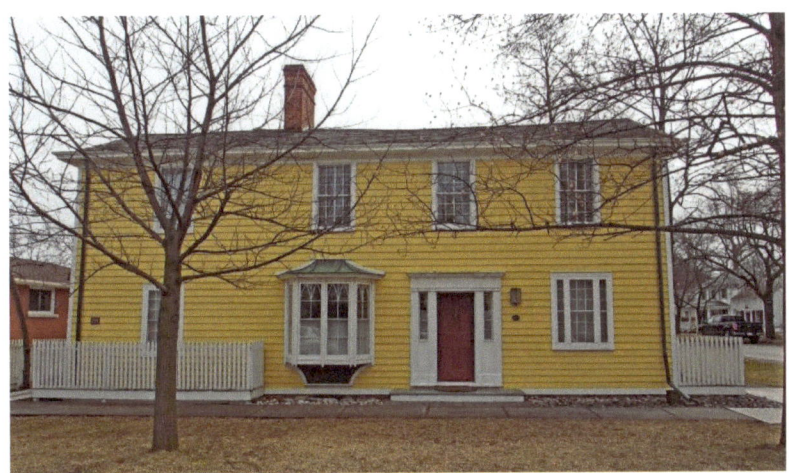

244 King Street c. 1828 – board and batten construction

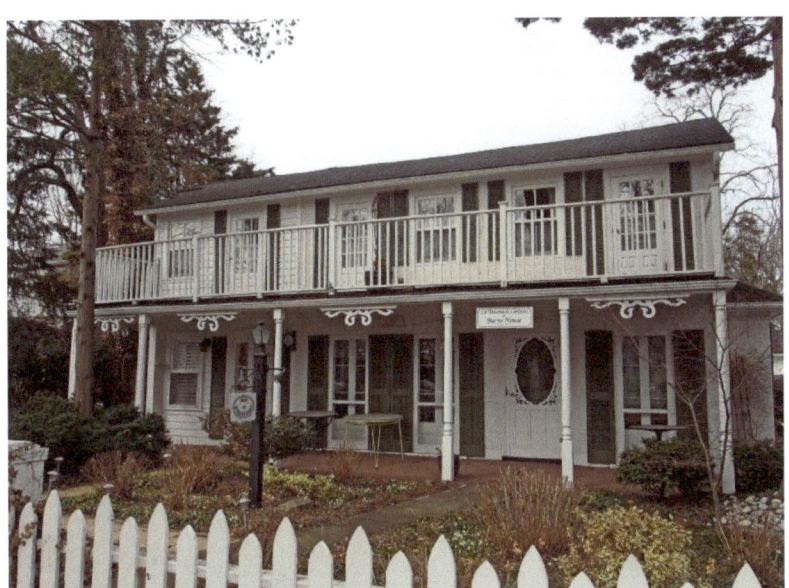

King Street – Burns House Bed and Breakfast c. 1818

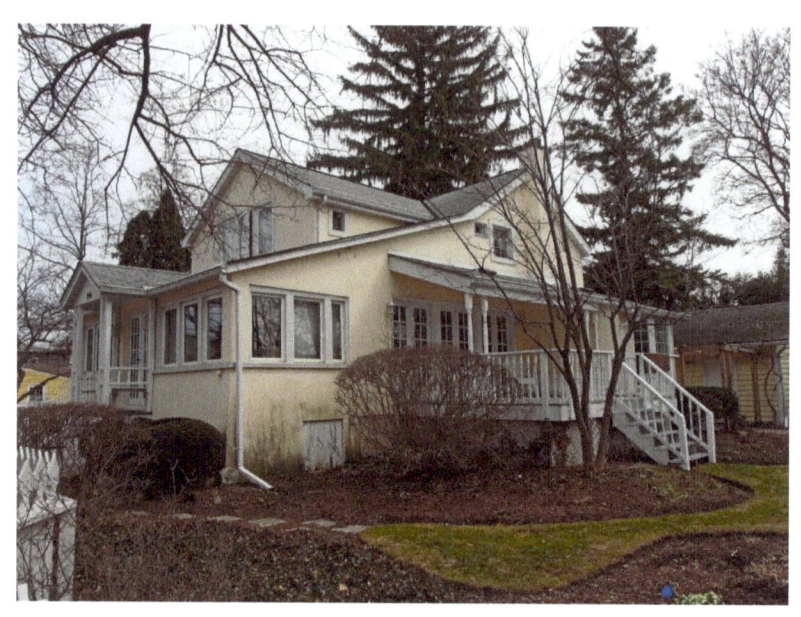

256 King Street - Gothic

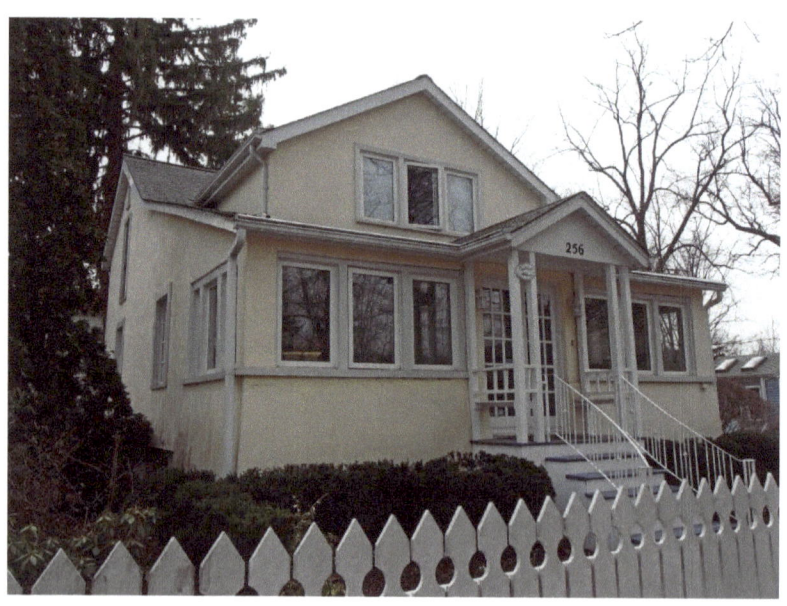

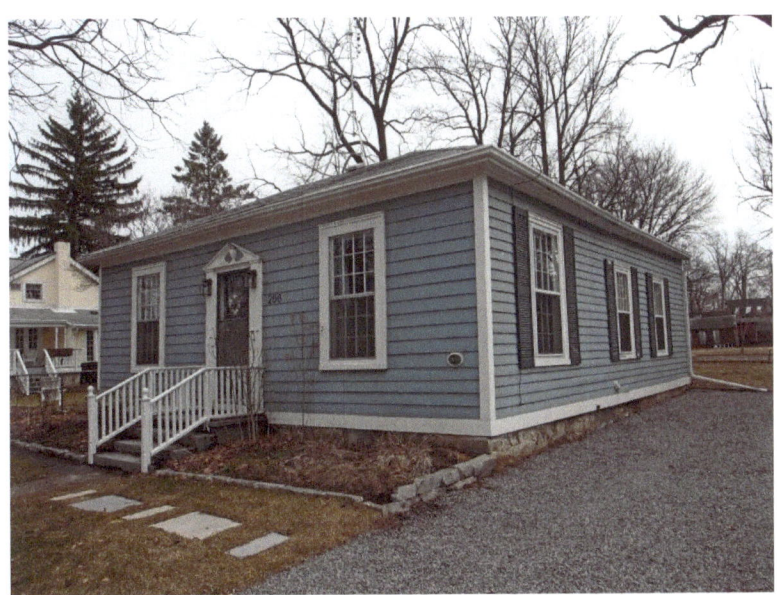

266 King Street c. 1849 – board and batten construction

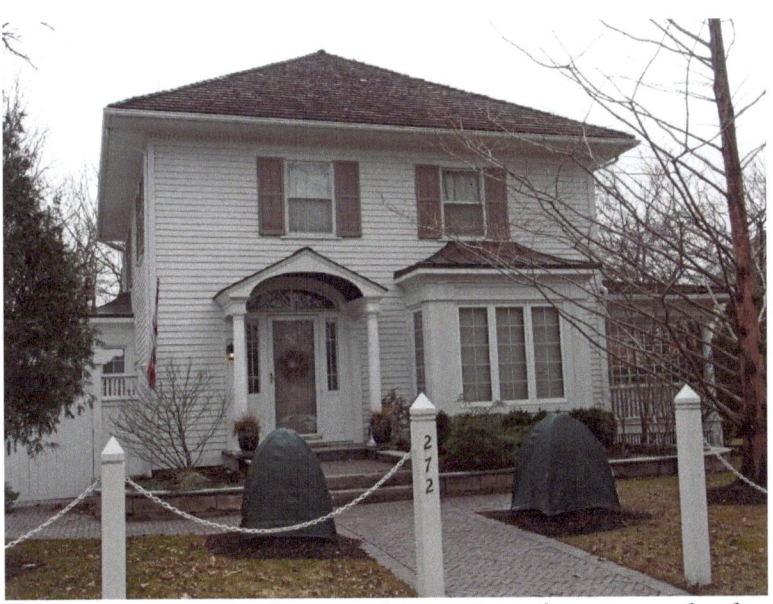

272 King Street – Italianate, hipped roof, rectangular bay window

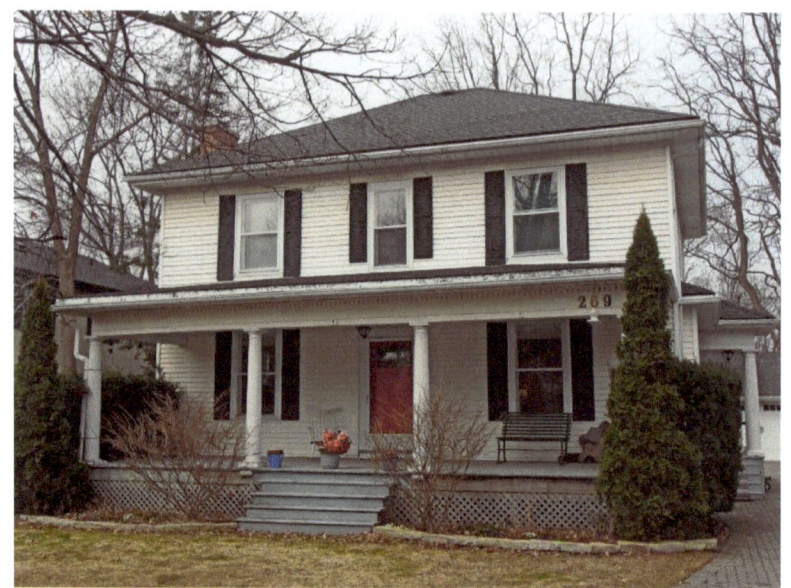

269 King Street – Italianate, hipped roof

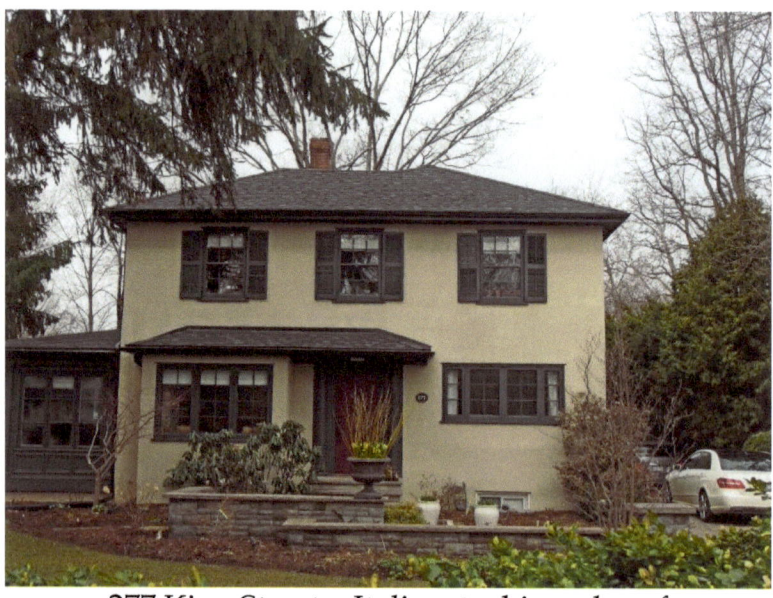

277 King Street – Italianate, hipped roof

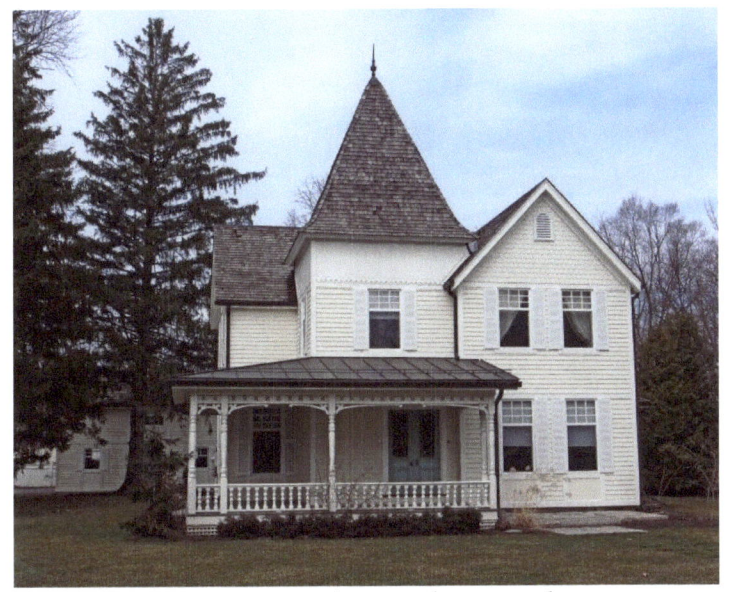

King Street – Gothic with central tower

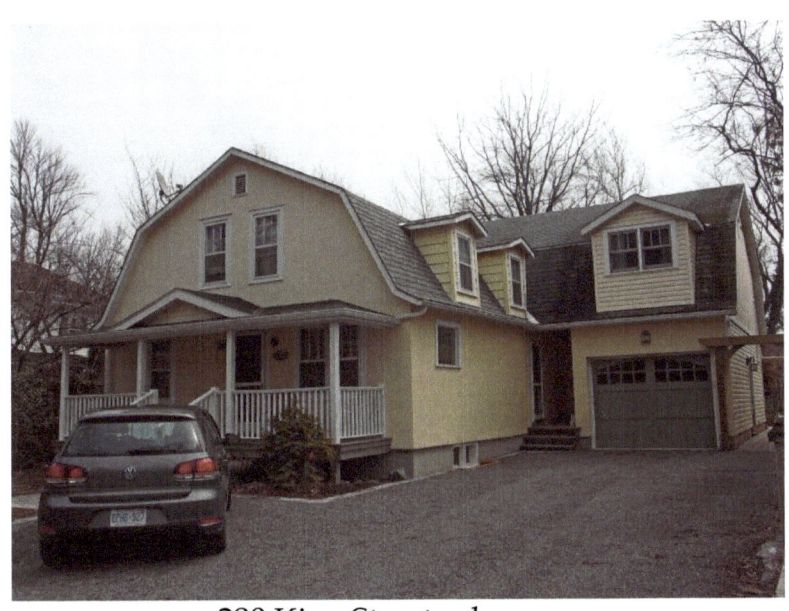

280 King Street - dormers

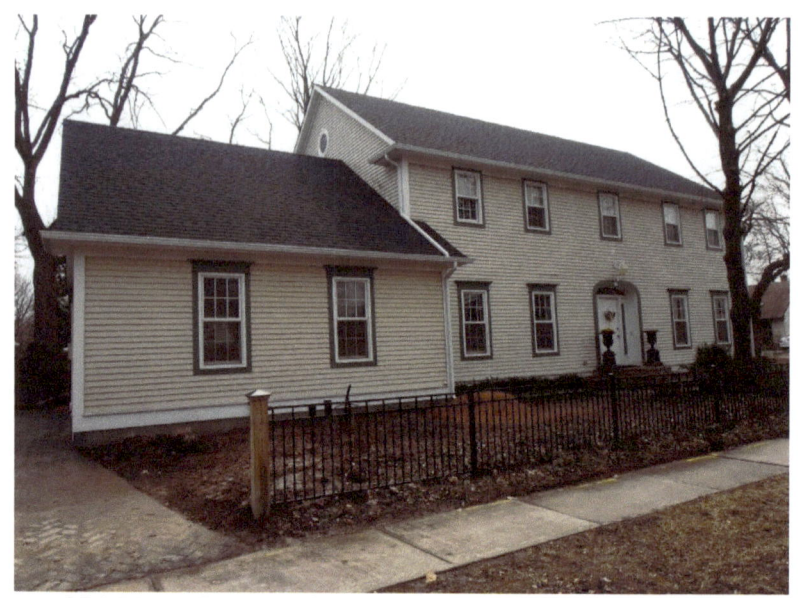

284 King Street – board and batten construction

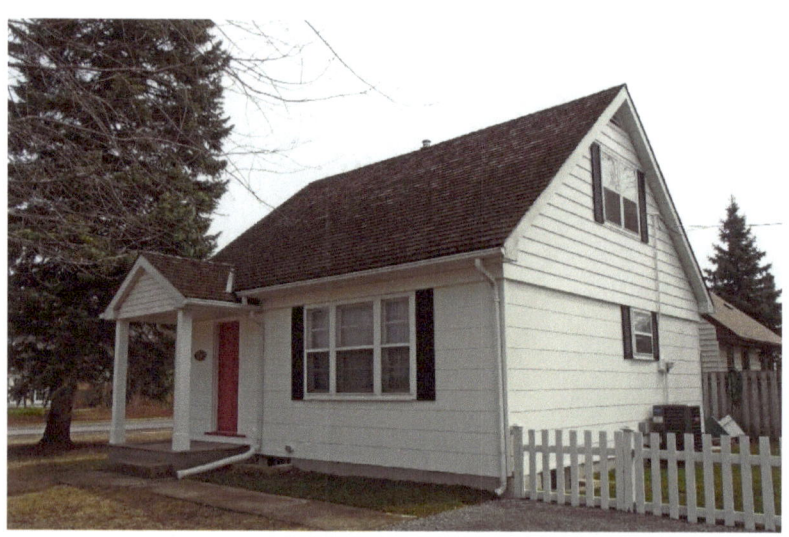

308 King Street

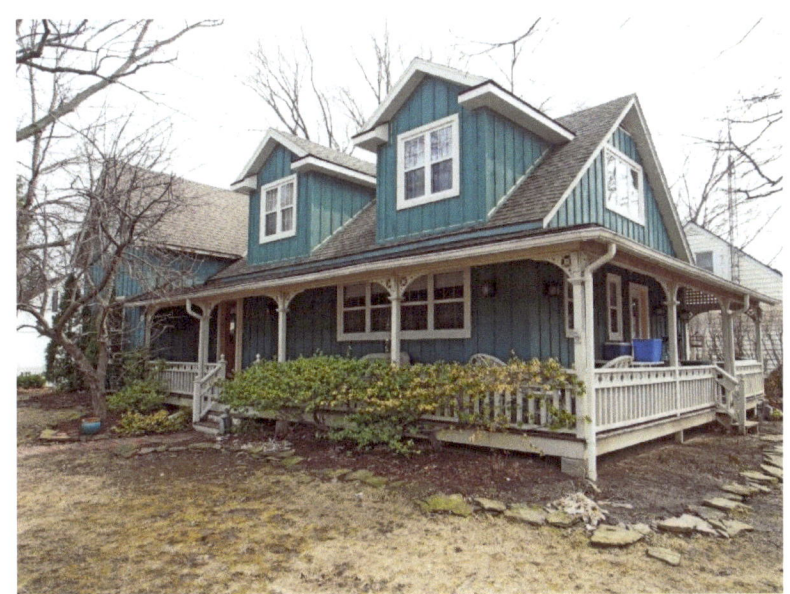

320 King Street – board and batten construction, dormers

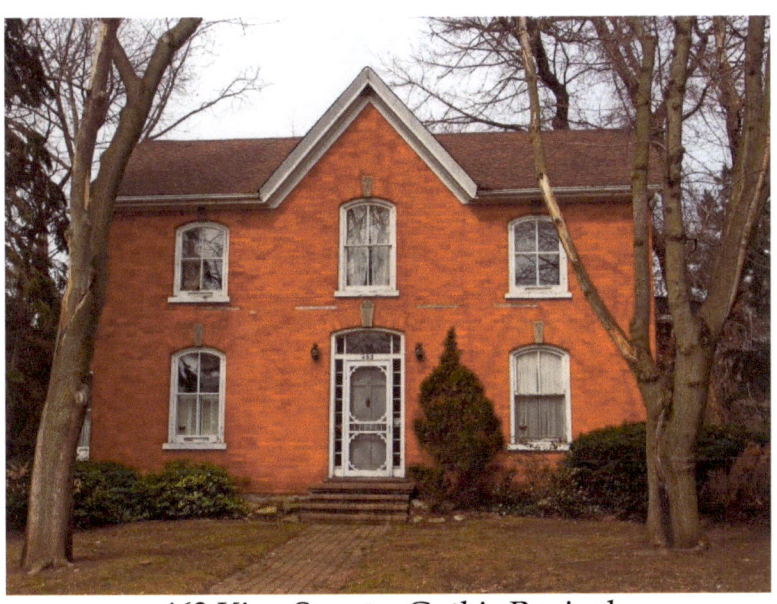

463 King Street – Gothic Revival

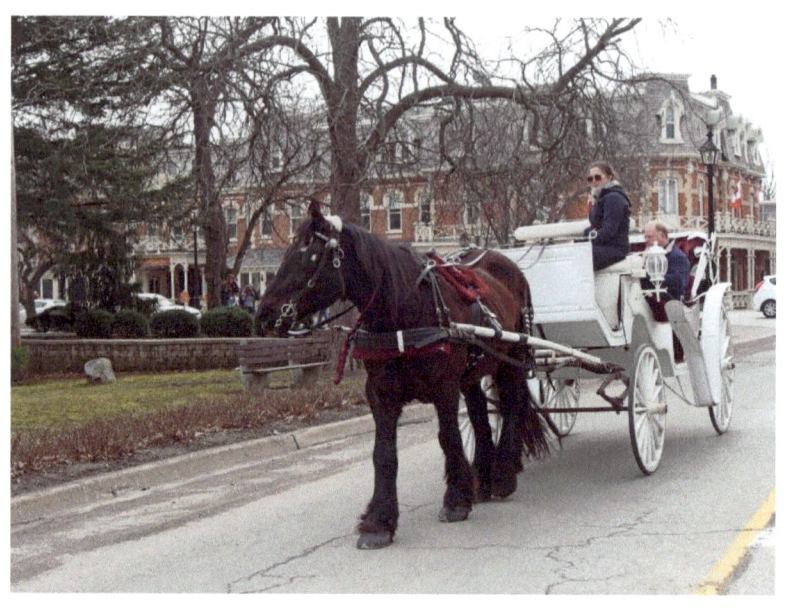

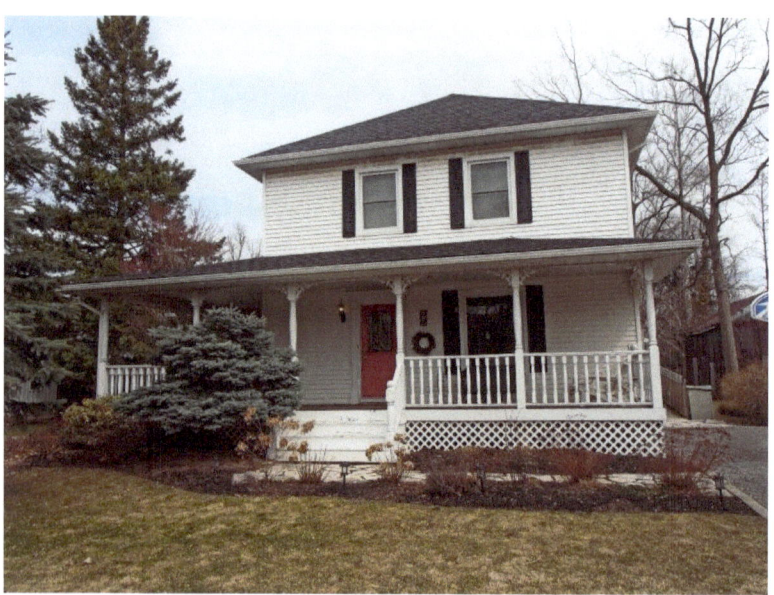

25 Castlereagh Street – hipped roof

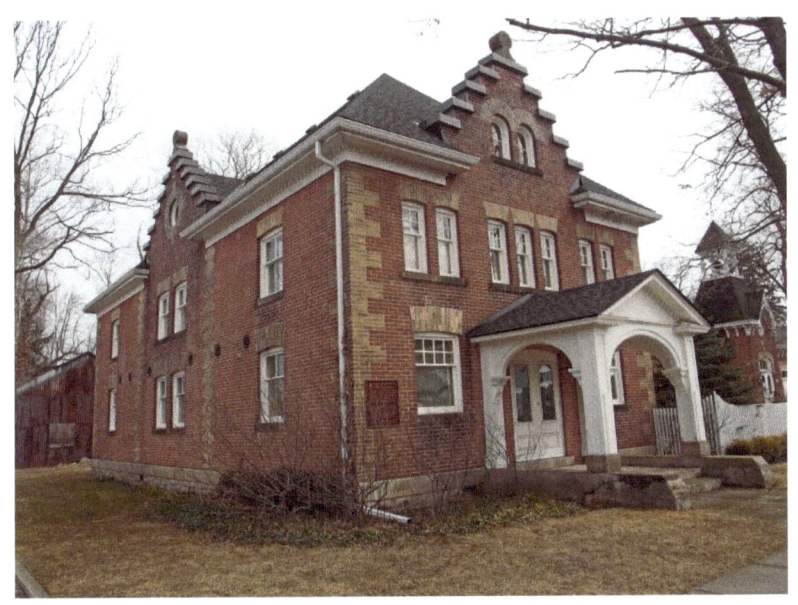

43 Castlereagh Street

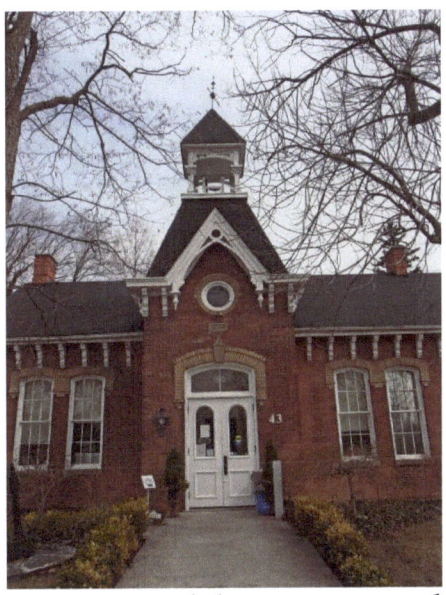

Cupola, voussoir with keystone over doorway,
transom window

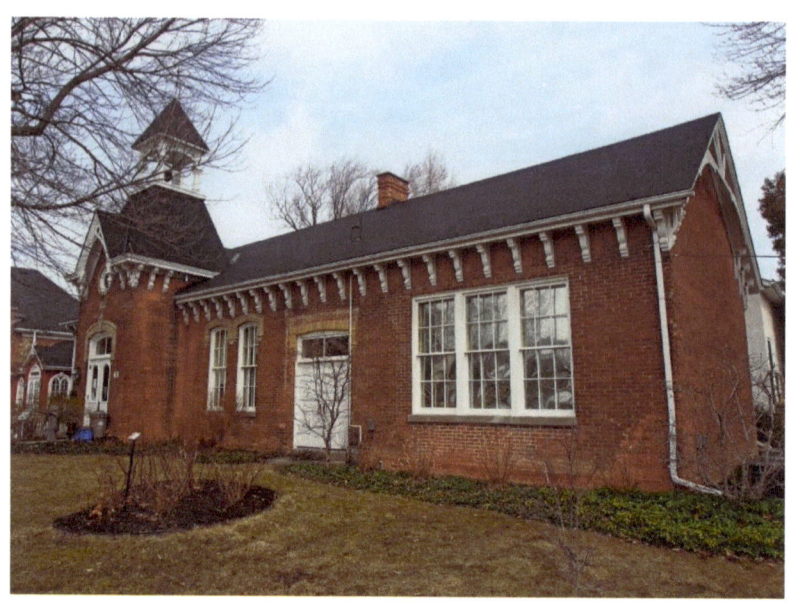

43 Castlereagh Street
Memorial Hall (1906) – the first building in Ontario to be
constructed solely as a historical museum
Cornice brackets under eaves, verge board trim on end gable

On July 20, 1799 the first edition of the *Canada Constellation*
was published at Niagara by Gideon and Silvester Tiffany,
two brothers who had come from the United States. Gideon
first held the post of King's Printer of Upper Canada, and with
Silvester edited the government-sponsored *Upper Canada
Gazette*. Suspected of American sympathies, the Tiffanys lost
their government support in 1797 and were succeeded by
Thomas Geer Simons. The Tiffanys subsequent efforts to
operate the *Canada Constellation* without government aid were
thwarted by limited population and the difficulty of collecting
subscriptions. The last issue appeared about July 1800.

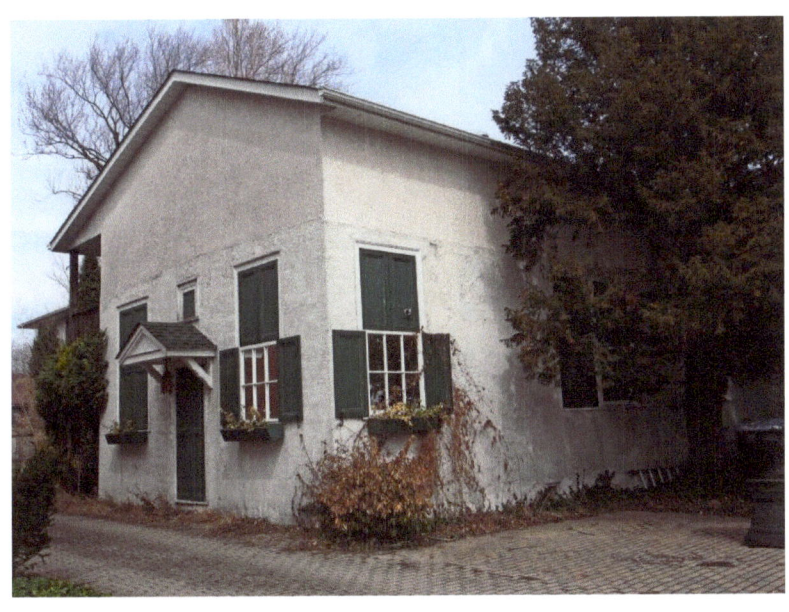

287 Davy Street – Blairpen House Country Inn

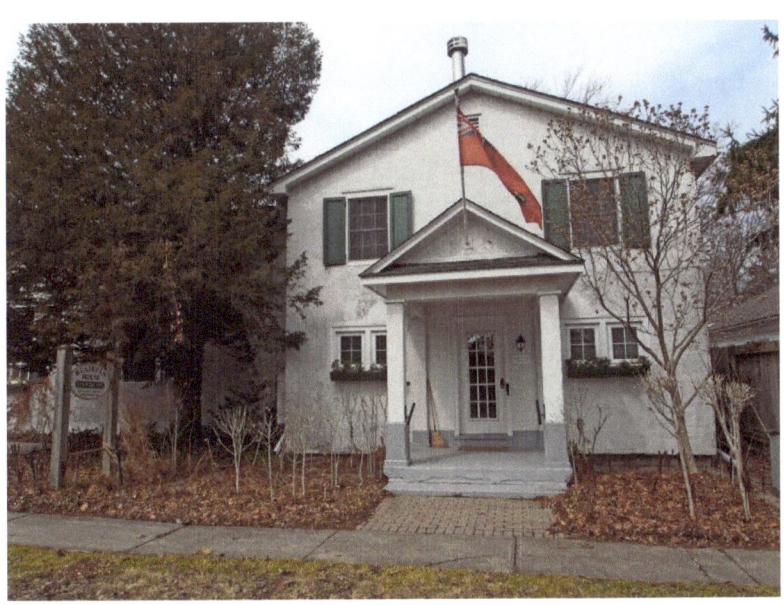

Pediment

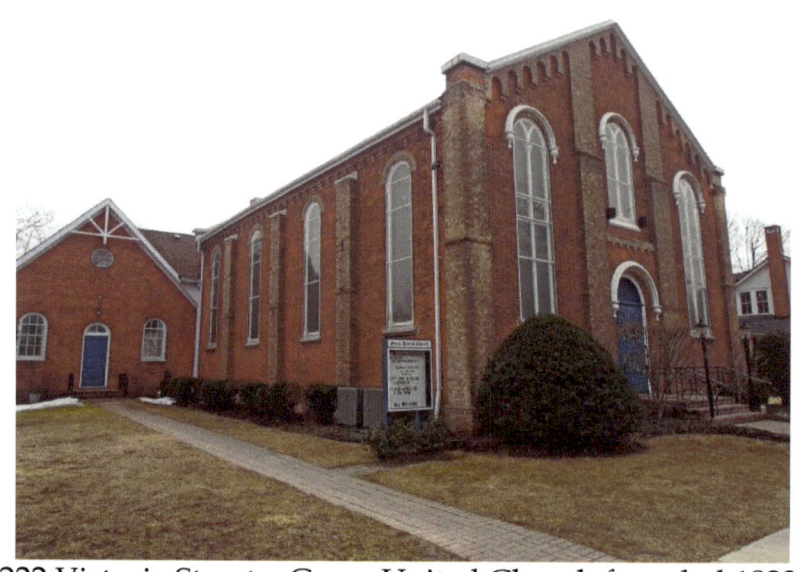

222 Victoria Street – Grace United Church founded 1823, building c. 1852 – buttresses, bevelled dentil moulding

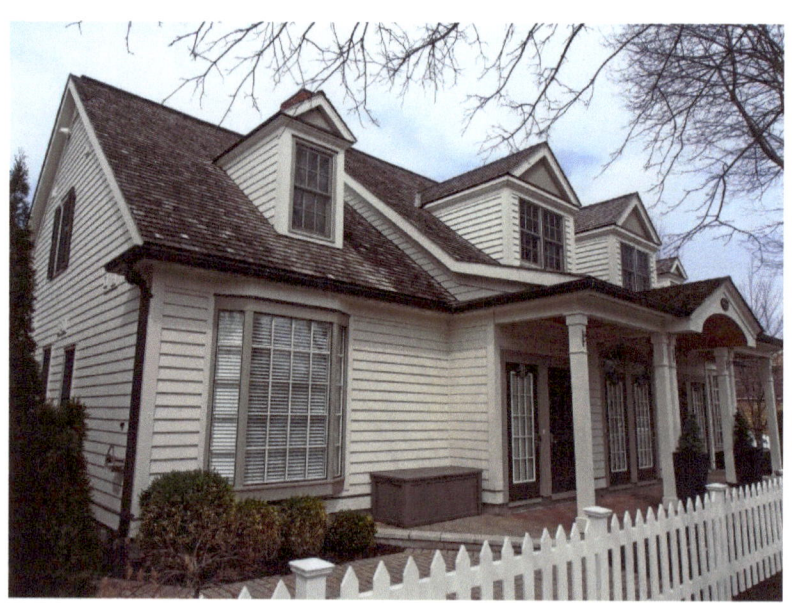

219 Victoria Street – The Caroline – built in 2001 - dormers

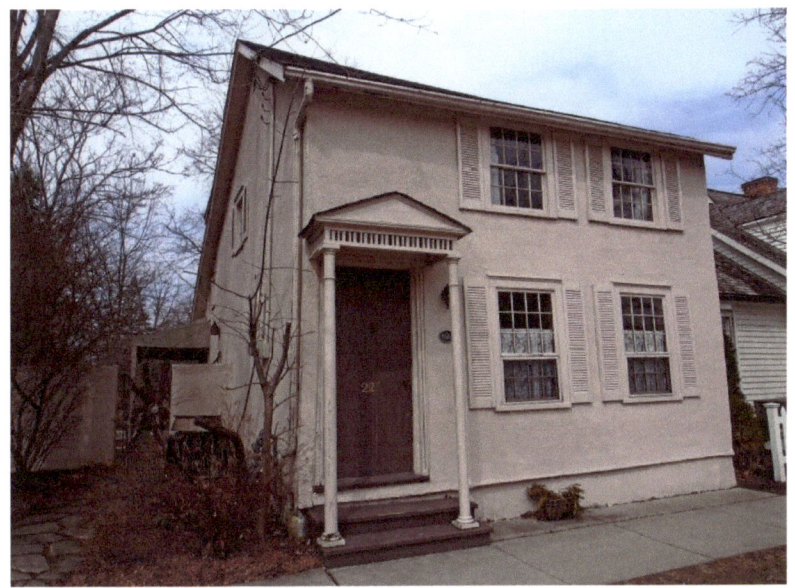

223 Victoria Street

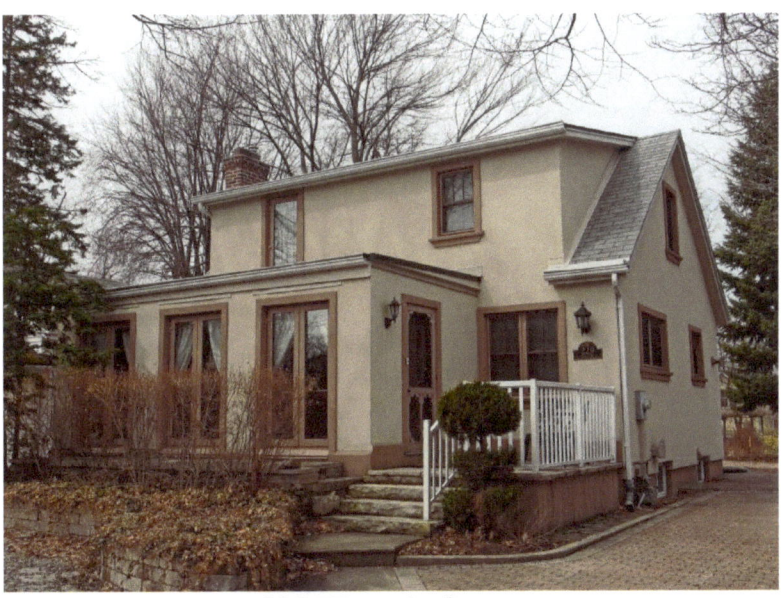

229 Victoria Street

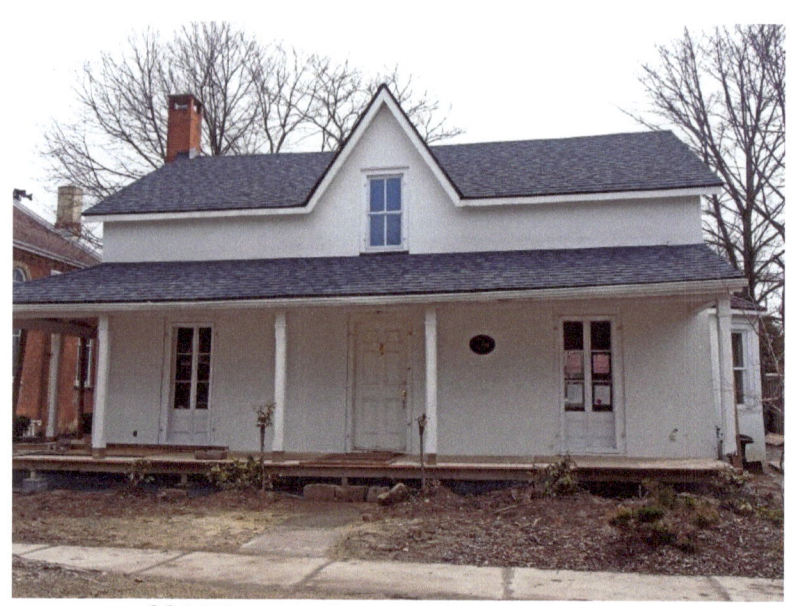

226 Victoria Street – Gothic Revival

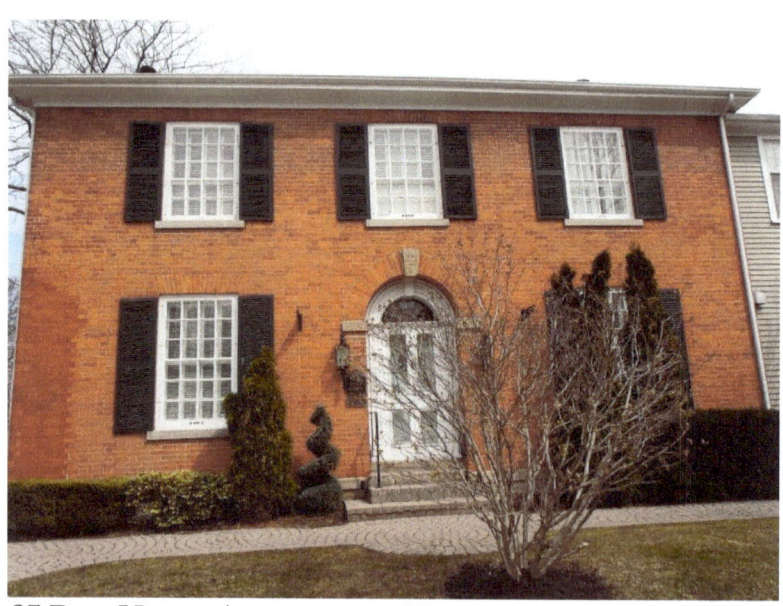

95 Post House (entrance on Victoria Street) - Georgian

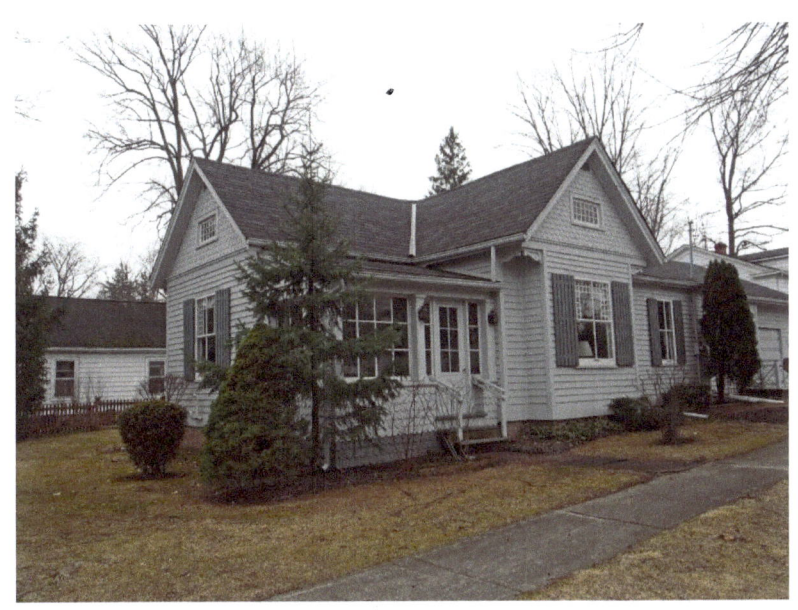

308 Victoria Street – Rose Cottage - Gothic

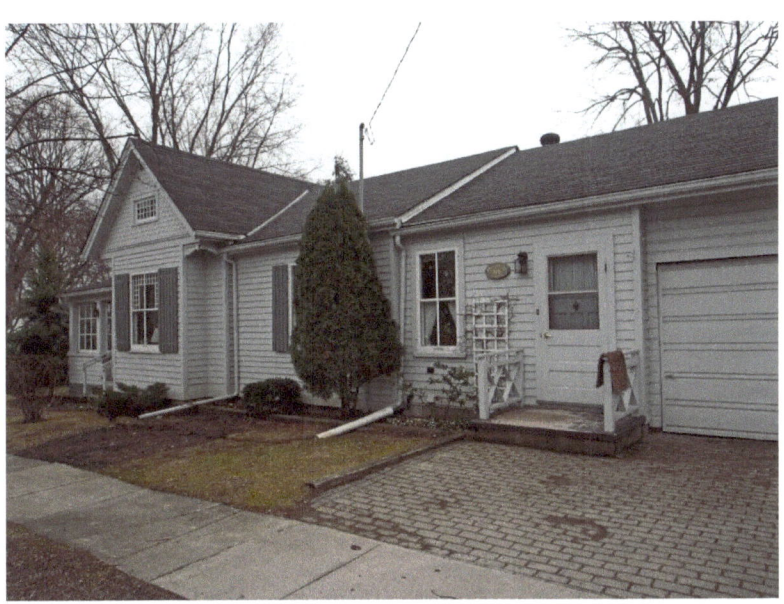

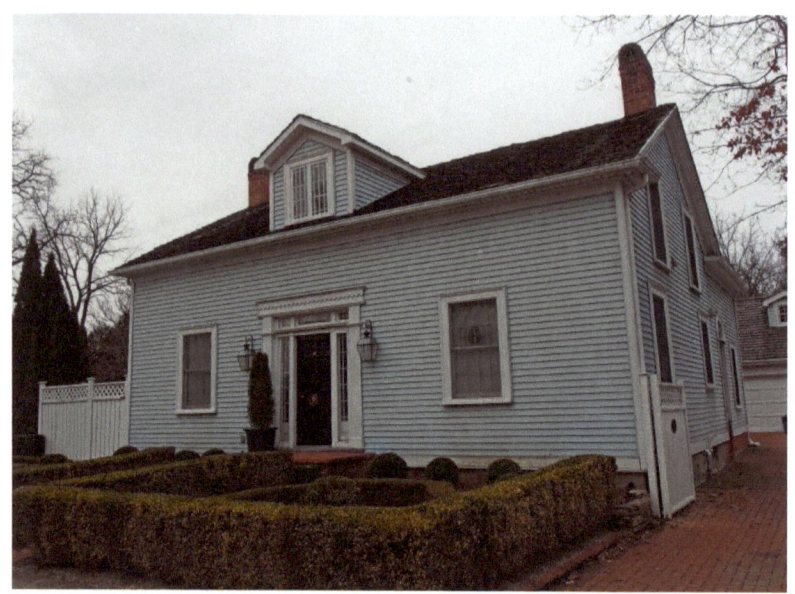

315 Victoria Street - dormer

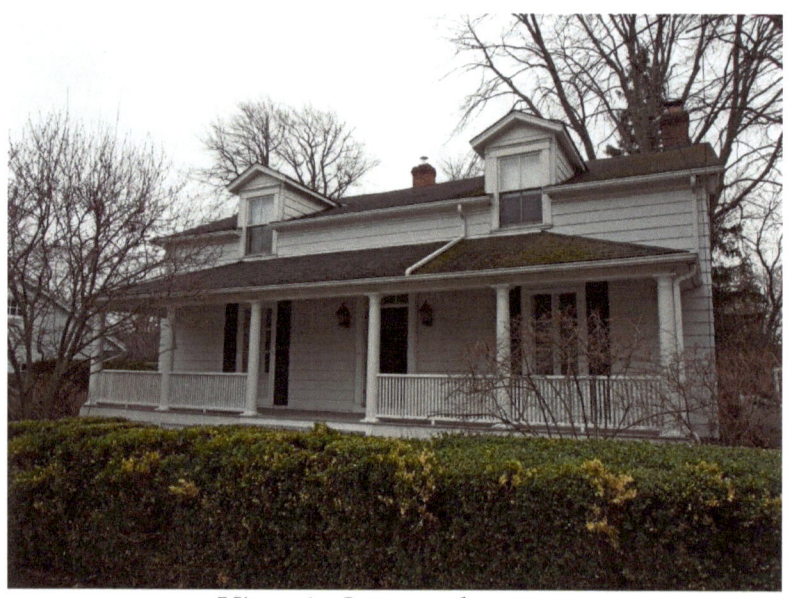

Victoria Street - dormers

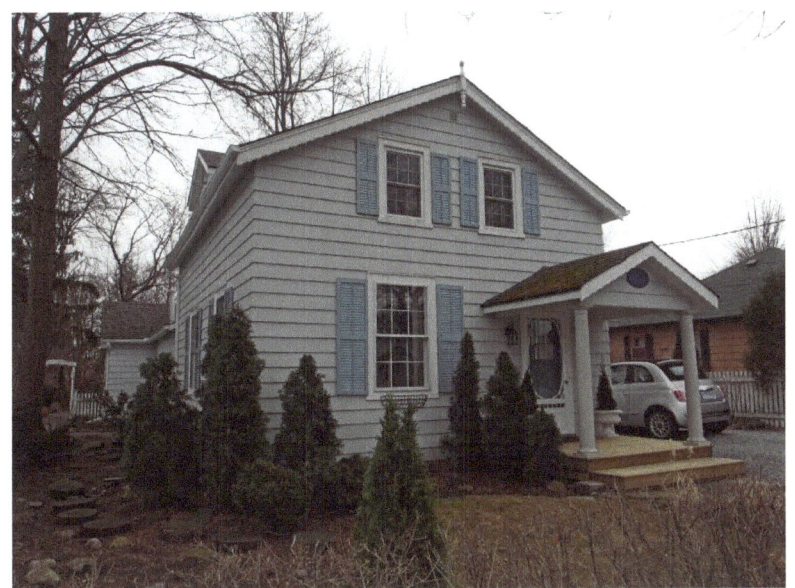

Victoria Street - Gothic

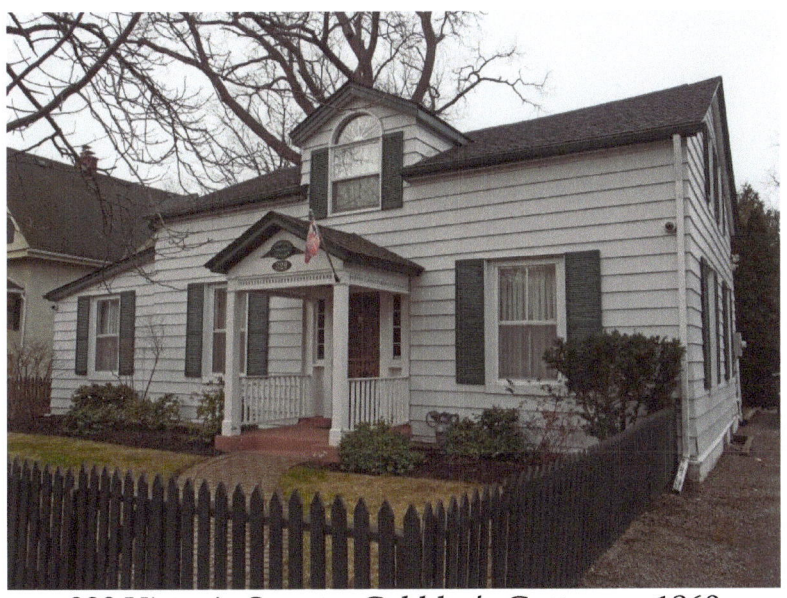

329 Victoria Street – Cobbler's Cottage c. 1860

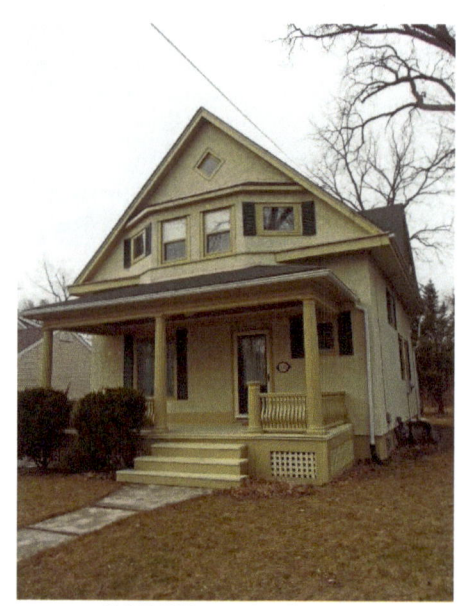

335 Victoria Street

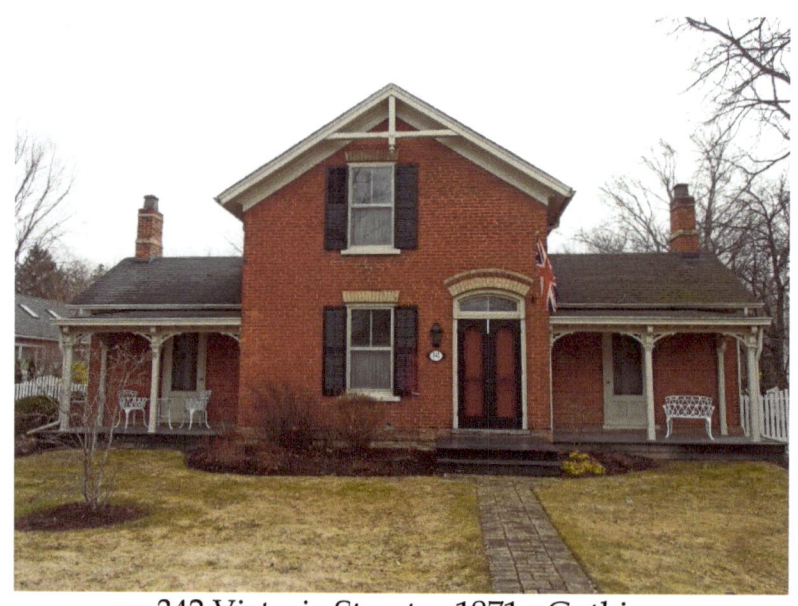

342 Victoria Street c. 1871 - Gothic

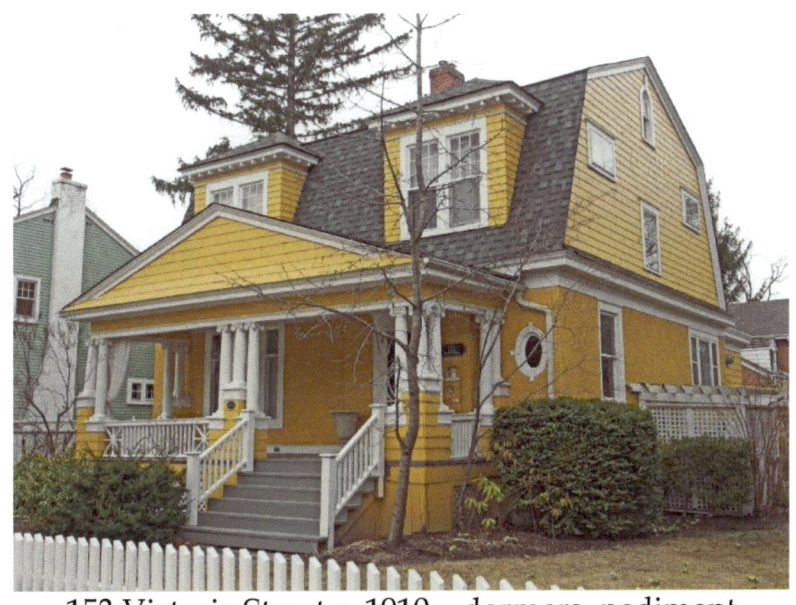

153 Victoria Street c. 1910 – dormers, pediment

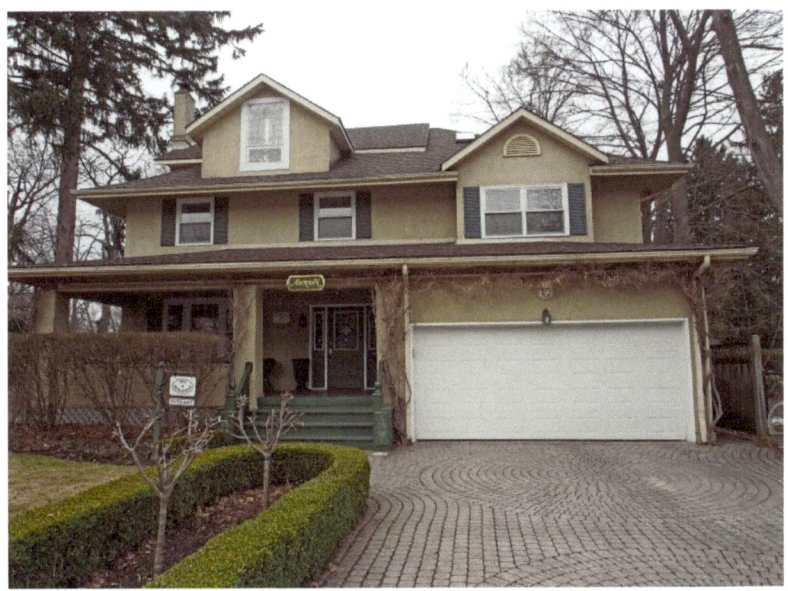

139 Victoria Street – Aberdeen Bed and Breakfast, dormers

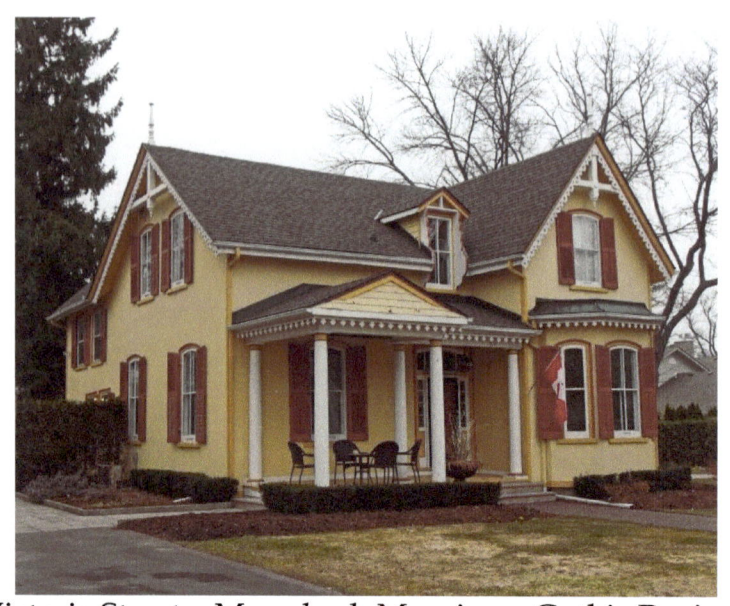

Victoria Street – Marrakech Mansion – Gothic Revival, verge board trim on gables, pediment, bay window

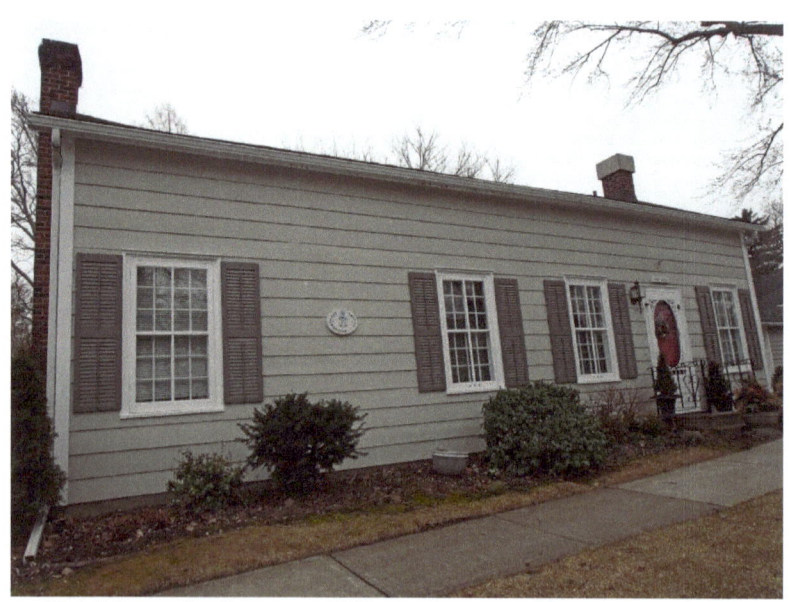

134 Victoria Street – Winterbottom Swayze c. 1835 – board and batten construction

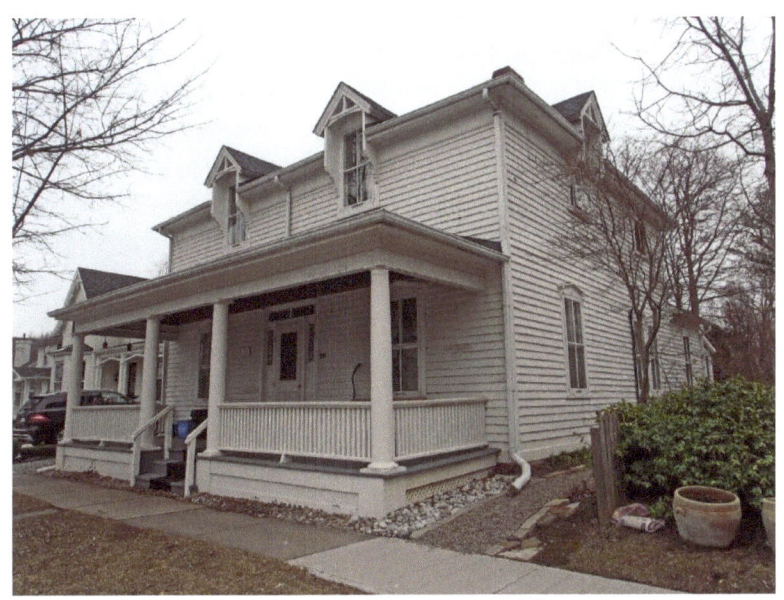

Victoria Street c. 1880

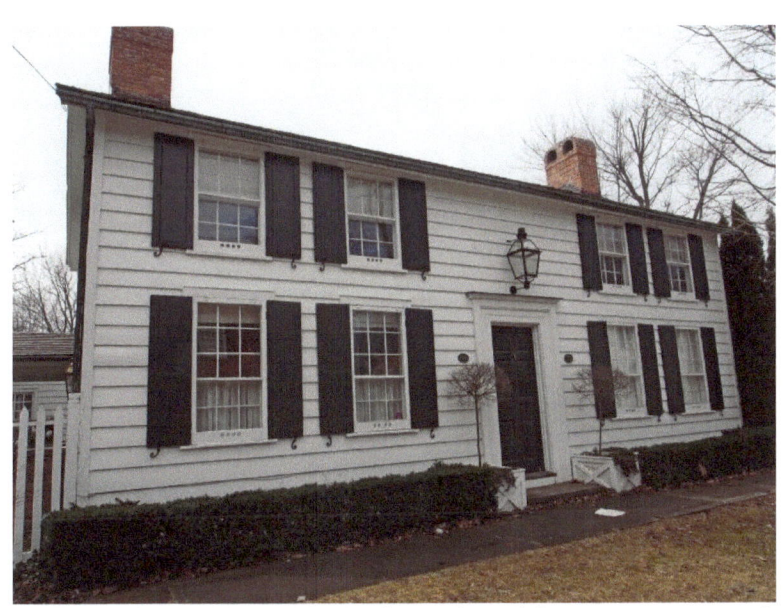

96 Johnson Street – c. 1816 – board and batten construction
Georgian style

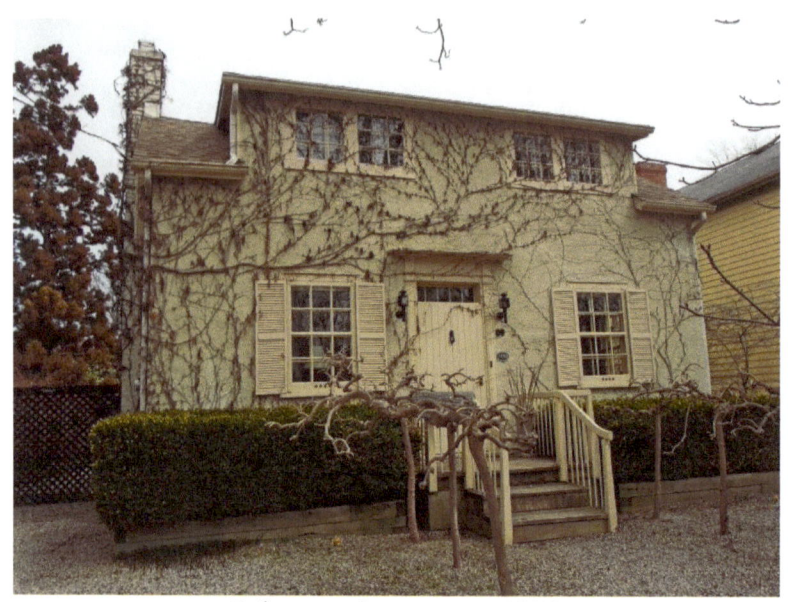

Johnson Street – c. 1850

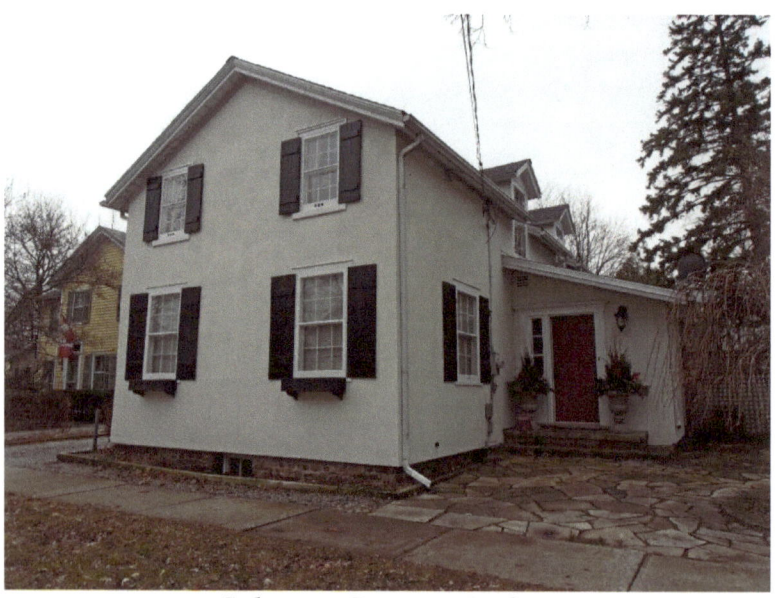

Johnson Street - Gothic

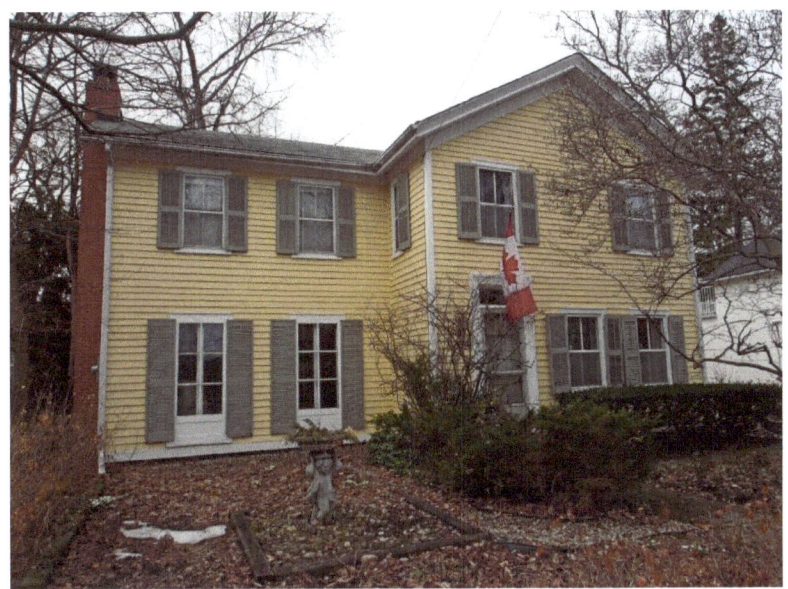

Johnson Street

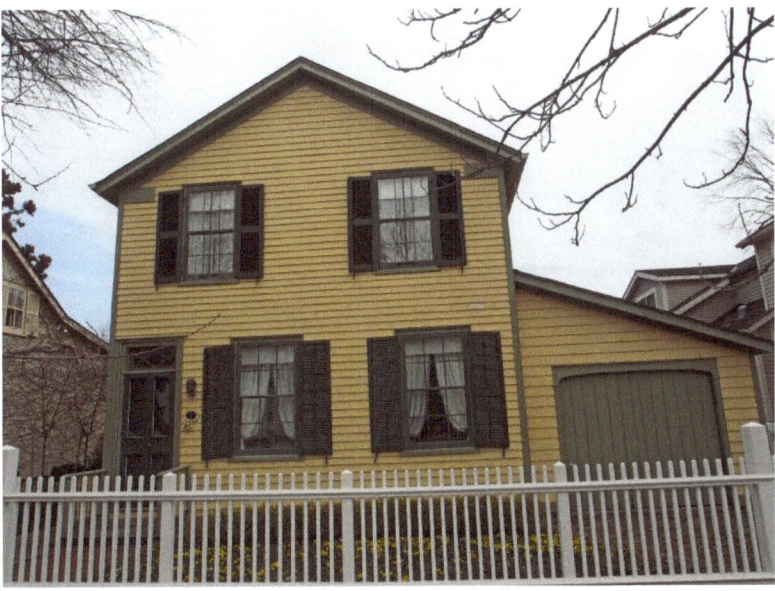

85 Johnson Street - Savage Scheffel House built 1843

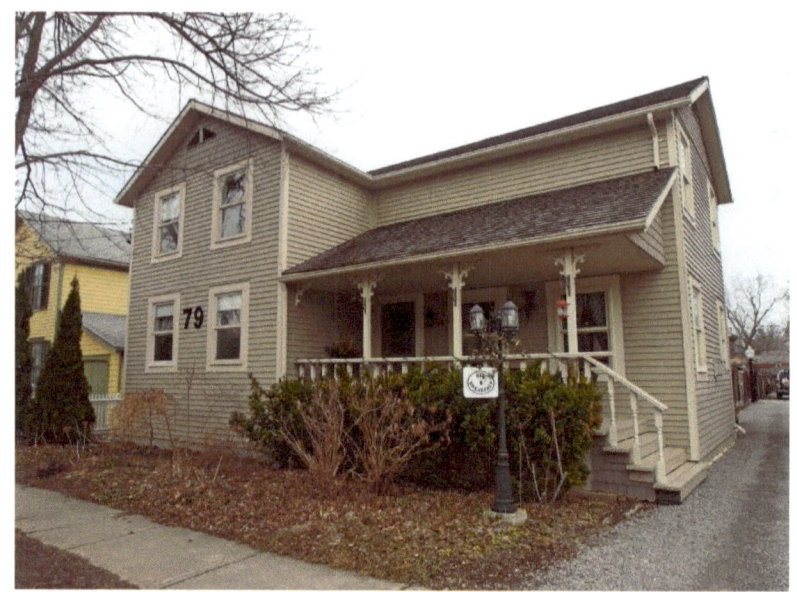

79 Johnson Street

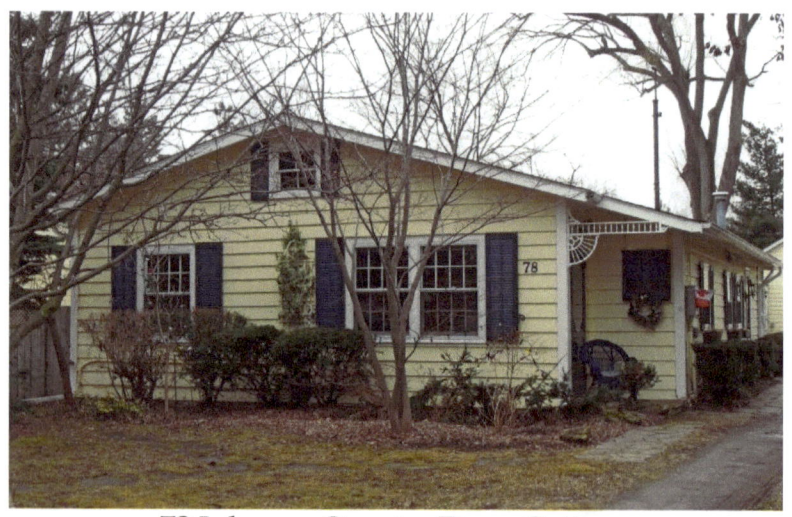

78 Johnson Street – Dory Cottage

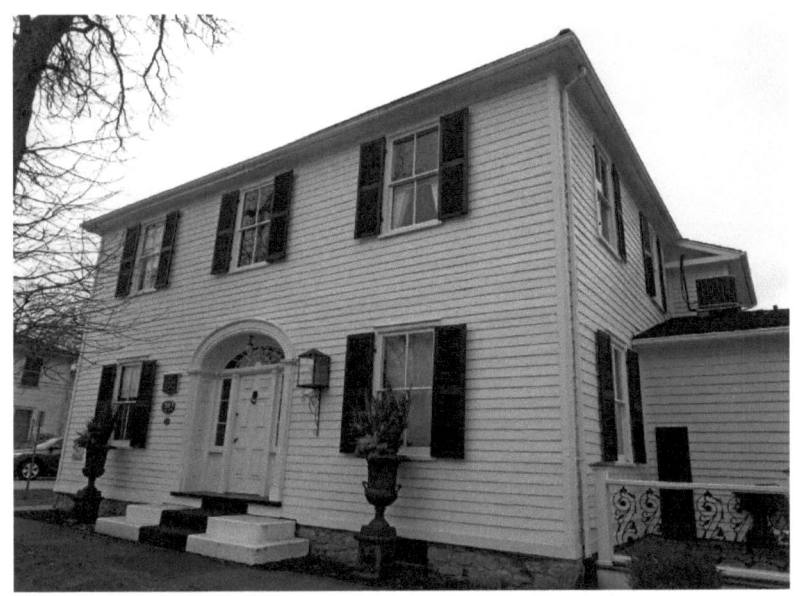

58 Johnson Street – Georgian residence

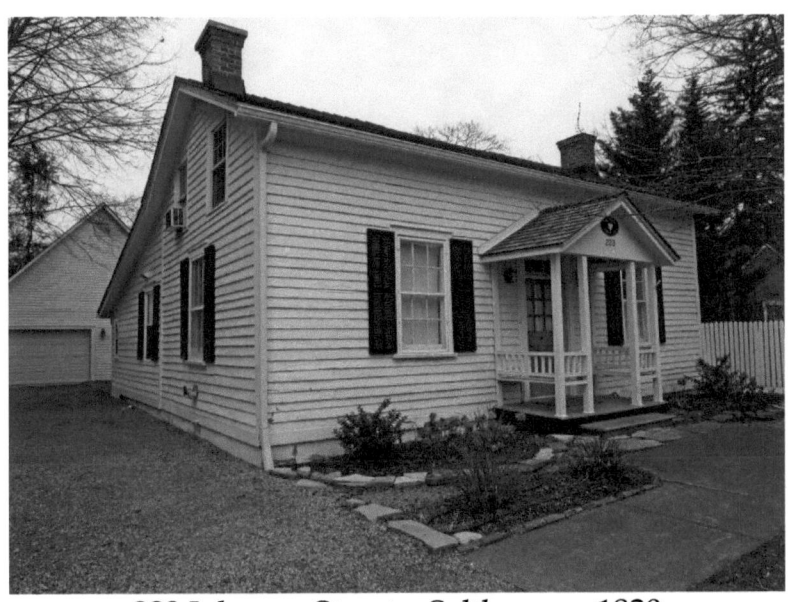

223 Johnson Street – Saltbox – c. 1820

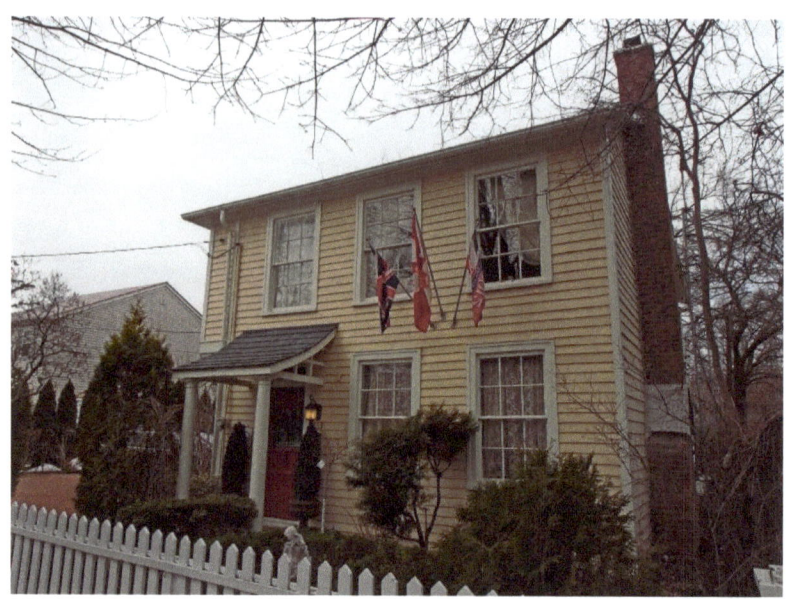

263 Regent Street

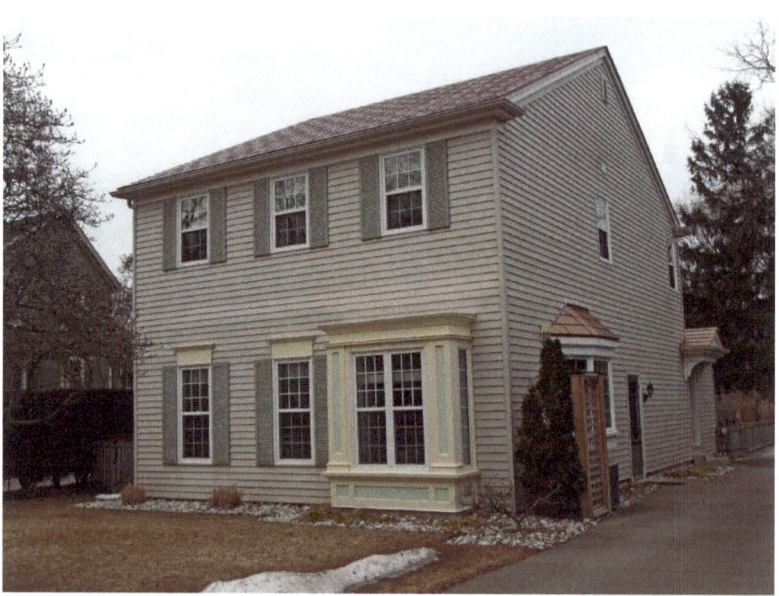

Regent Street - – board and batten construction

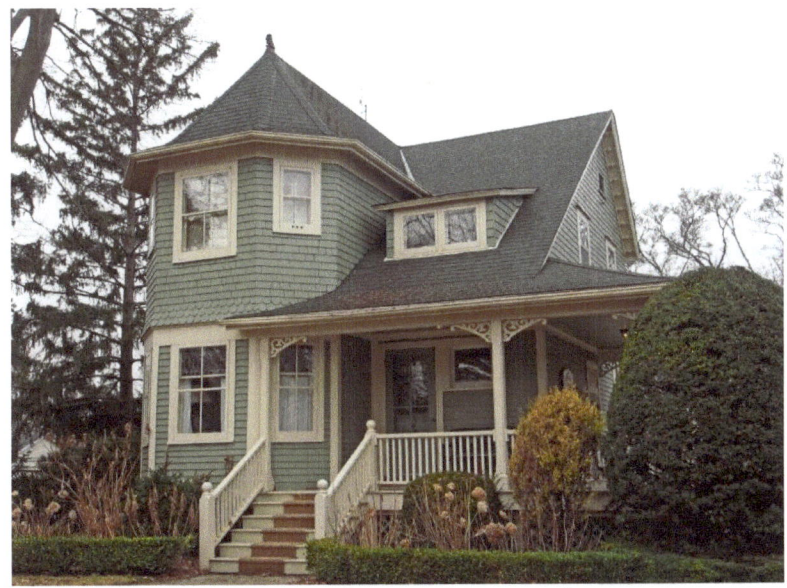

Regent Street – Queen Anne style, turret

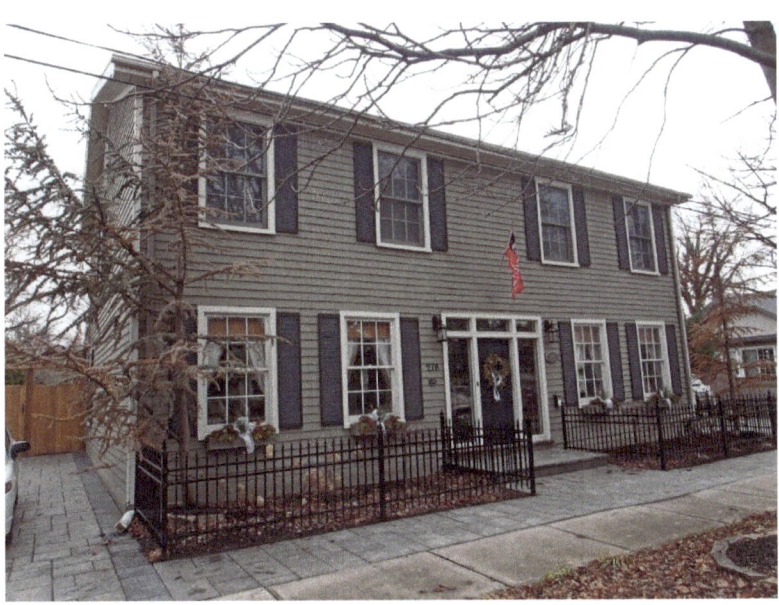

278 Regent Street – Regent House c. 1836 – Georgian
– board and batten construction

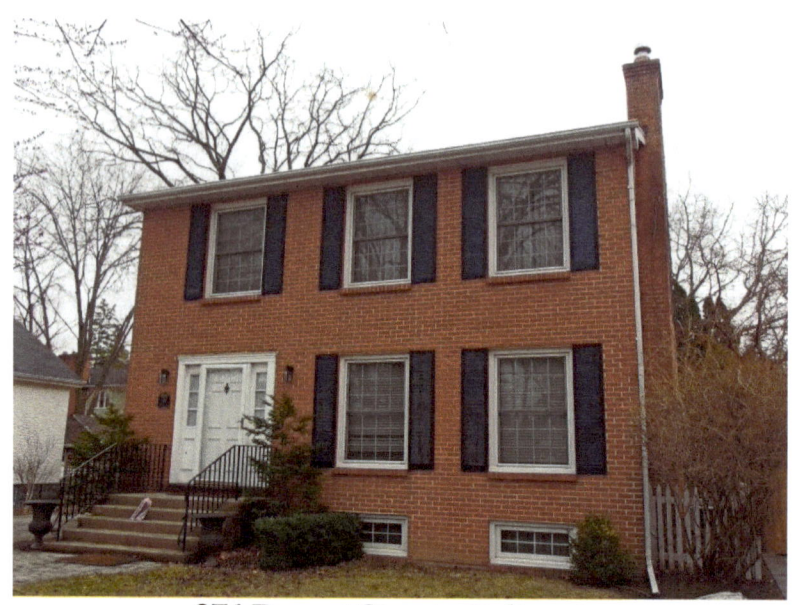

276 Regent Street - Italianate

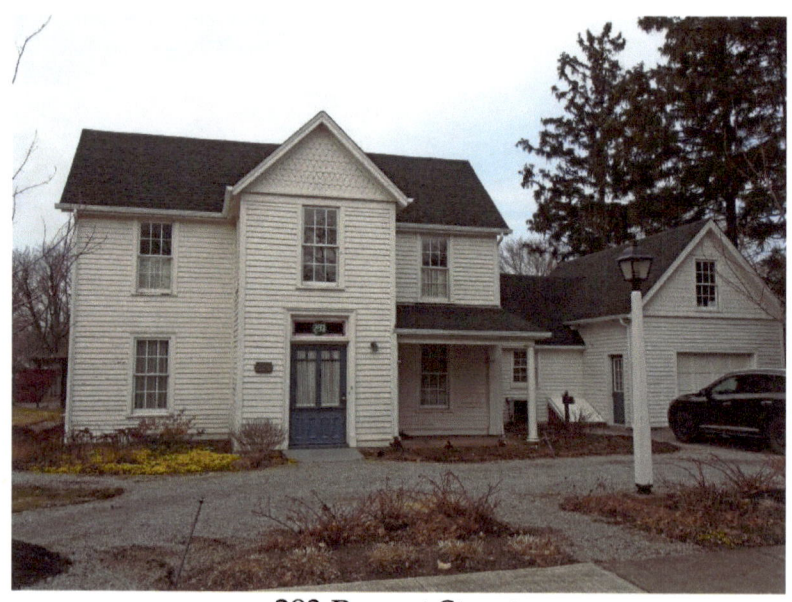

293 Regent Street

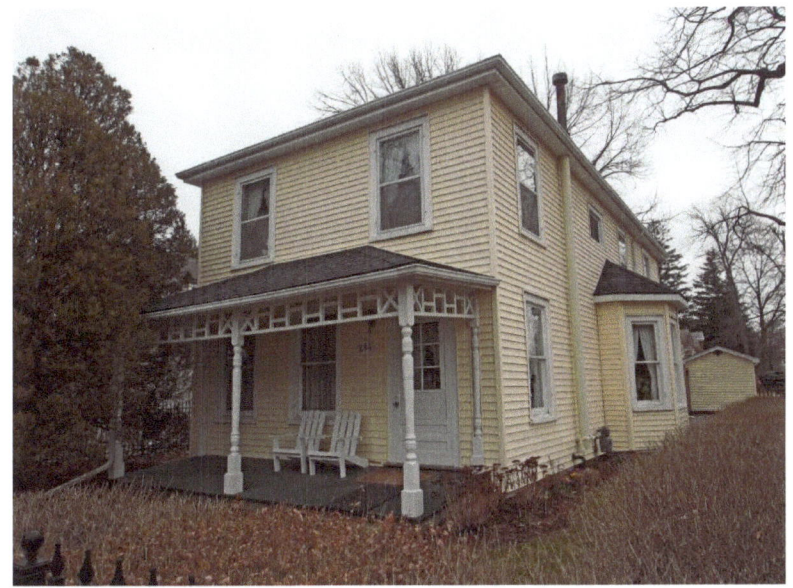

294 Regent Street – bay window on side
– board and batten construction

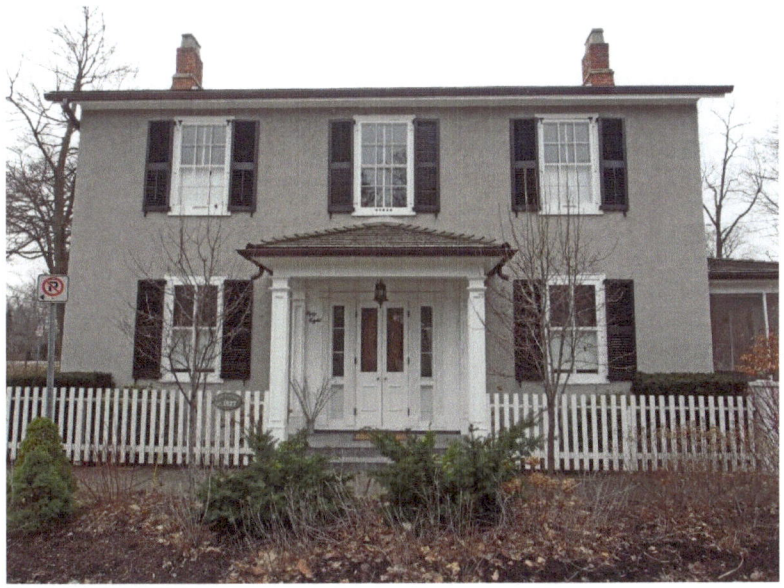

58 Gage Street – Taylor House c. 1827 - Georgian

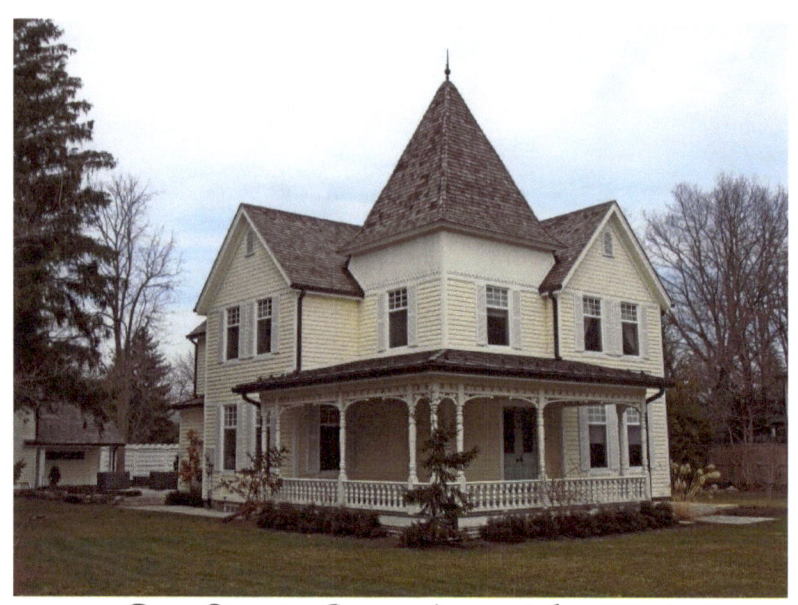

Gage Street – Queen Anne style, turret

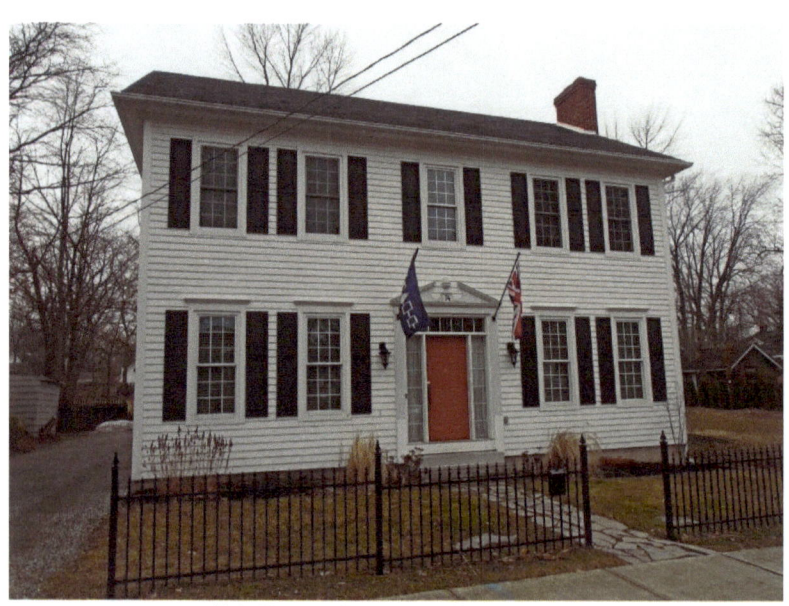

74 Gage Street - Georgian

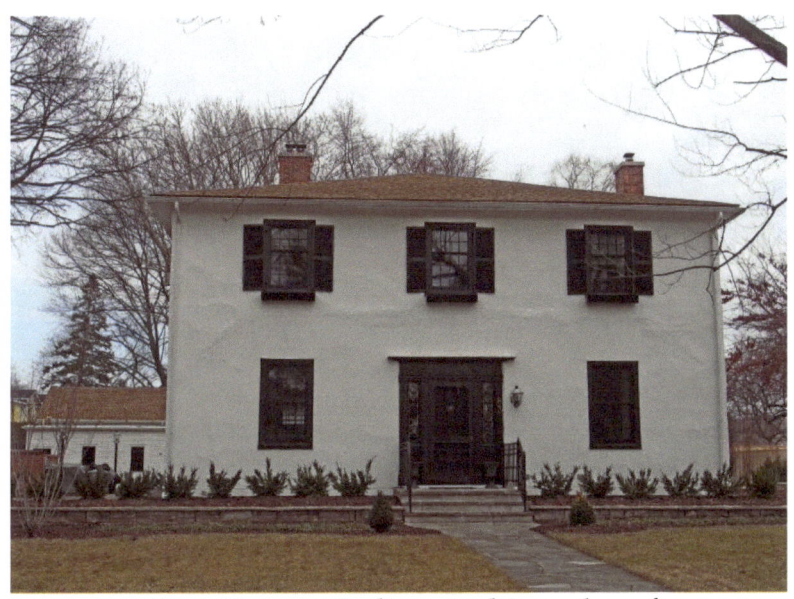

Gage Street – Italianate, hipped roof

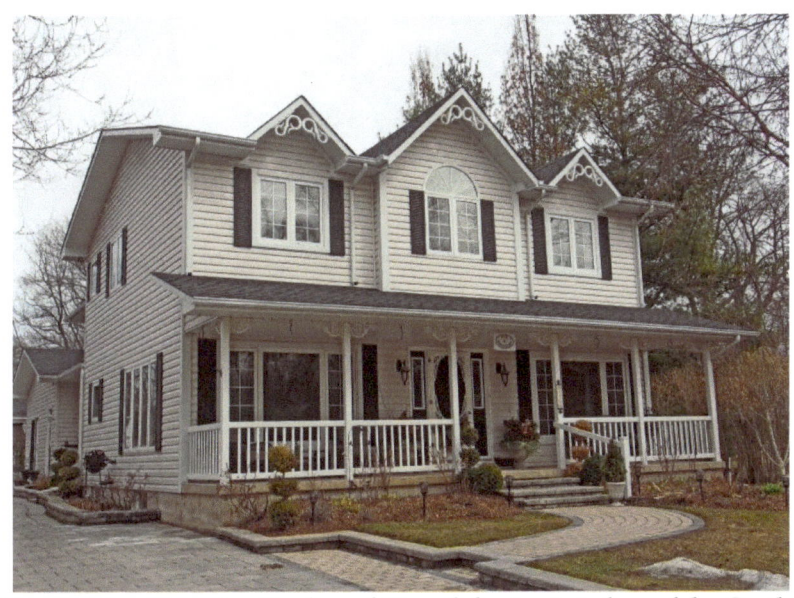

125 Centre Street – Bed and Breakfast – triple gable Gothic Revival, verge board on gables

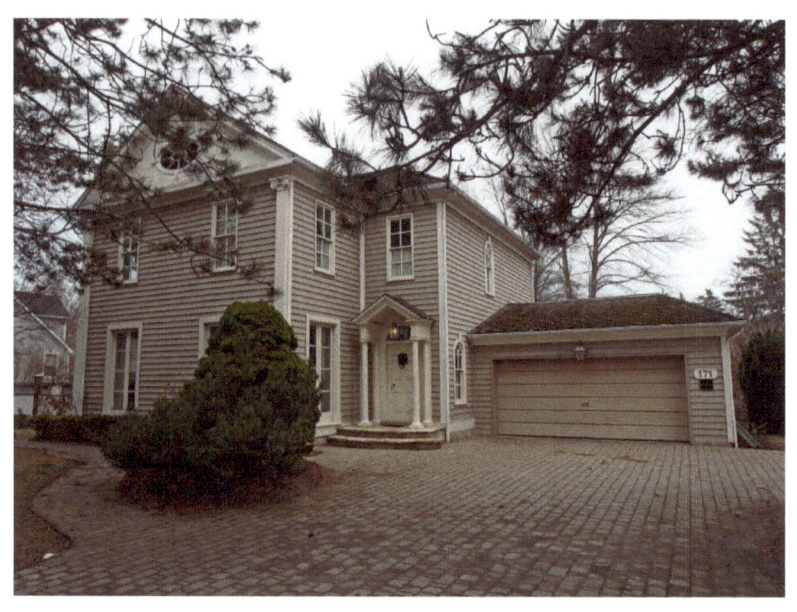

171 Centre Street – The Lions' Den

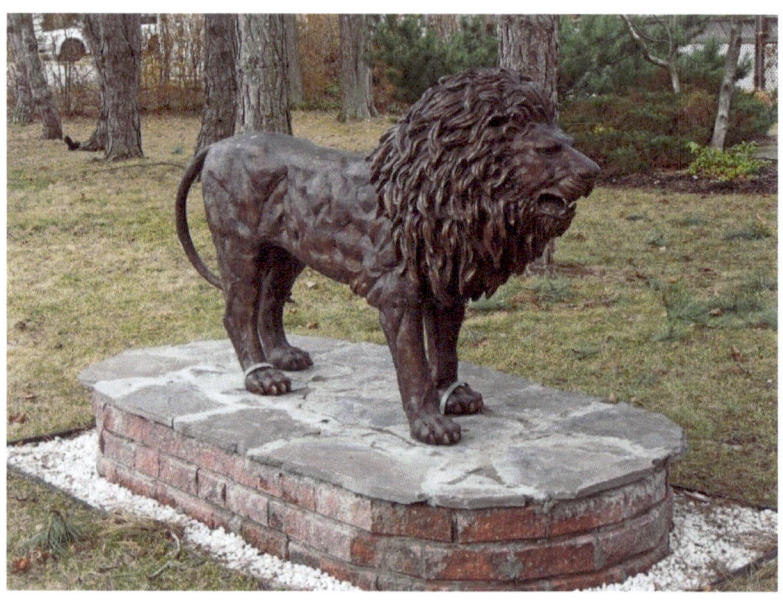

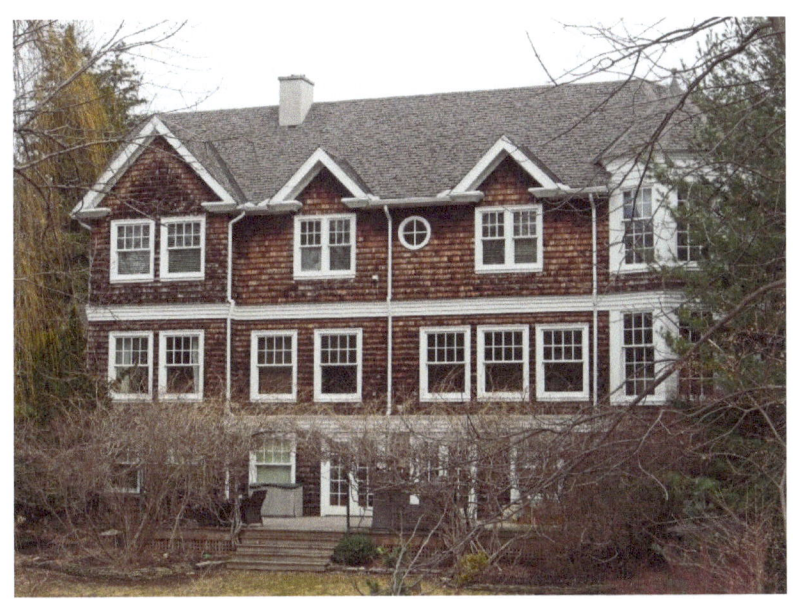

Centre Street – Gothic – cornice return on gables

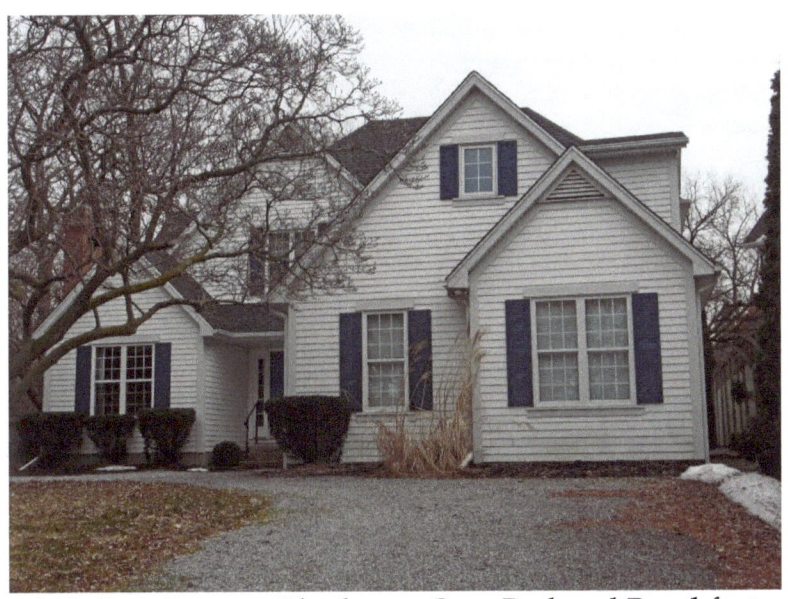

330 Gate Street – Blueberry Gate Bed and Breakfast

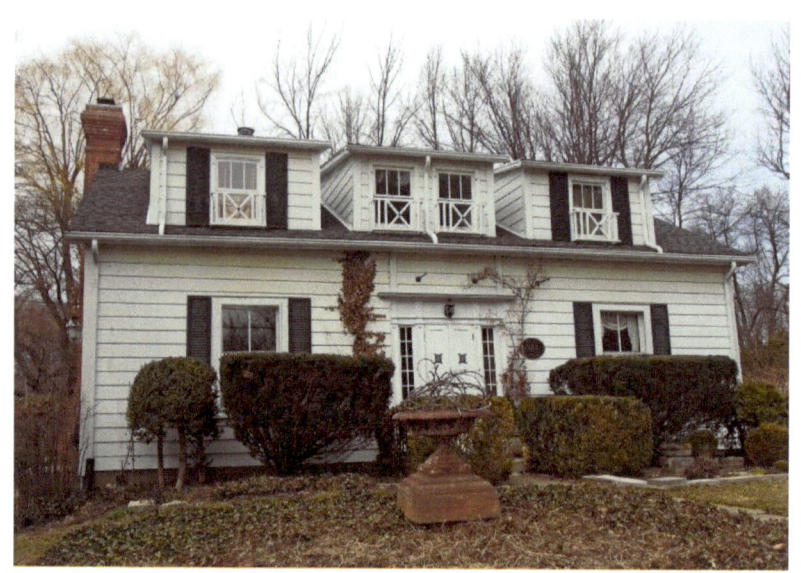

323 Gate Street - dormers

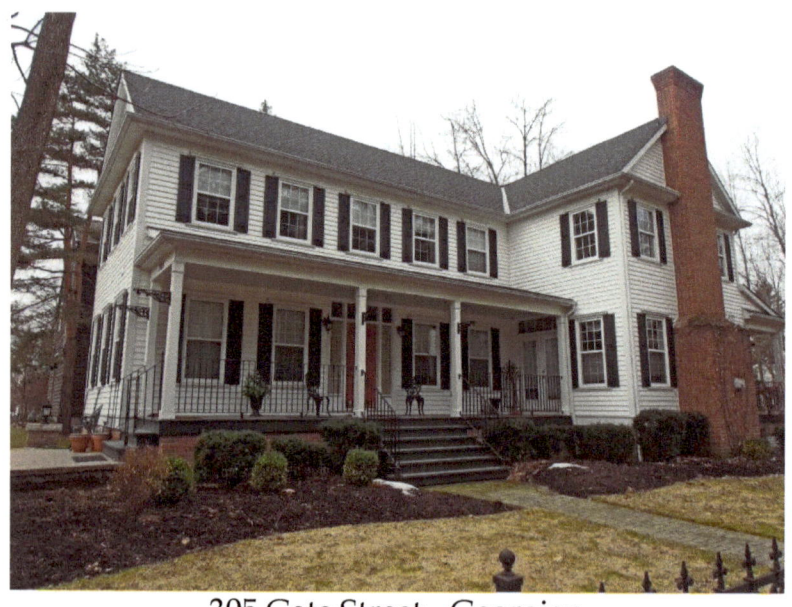

305 Gate Street - Georgian

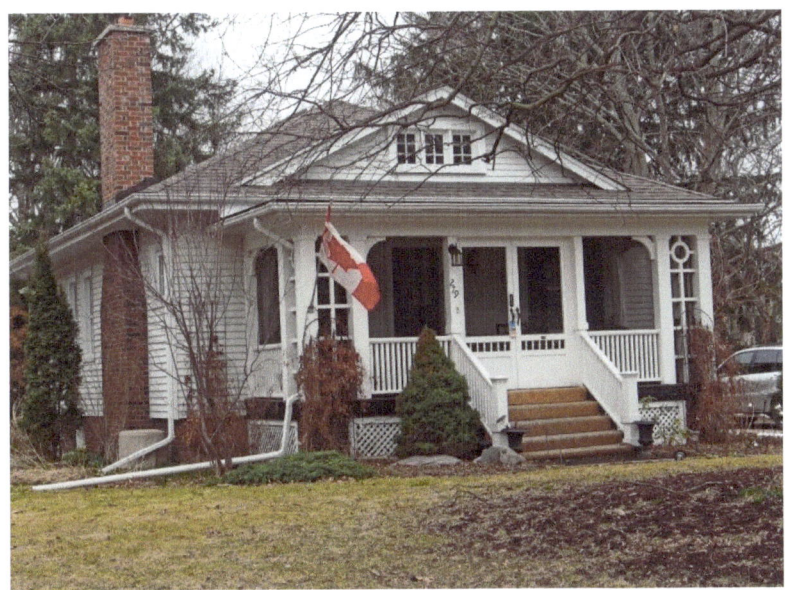

279 Gate Street

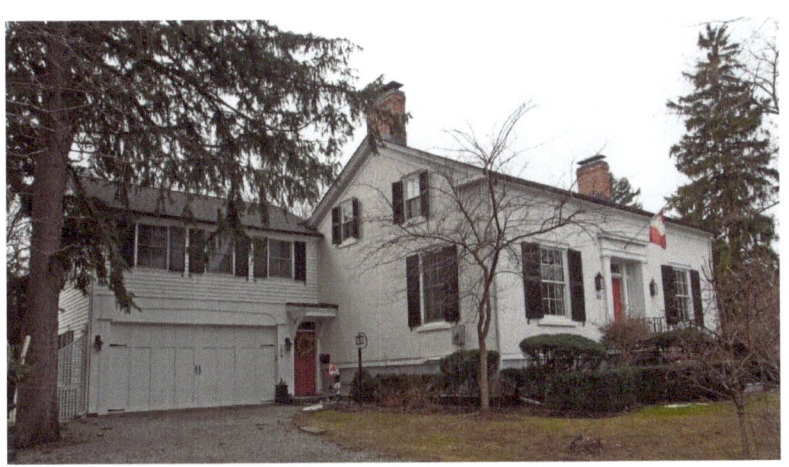

274 Gate Street - Gothic

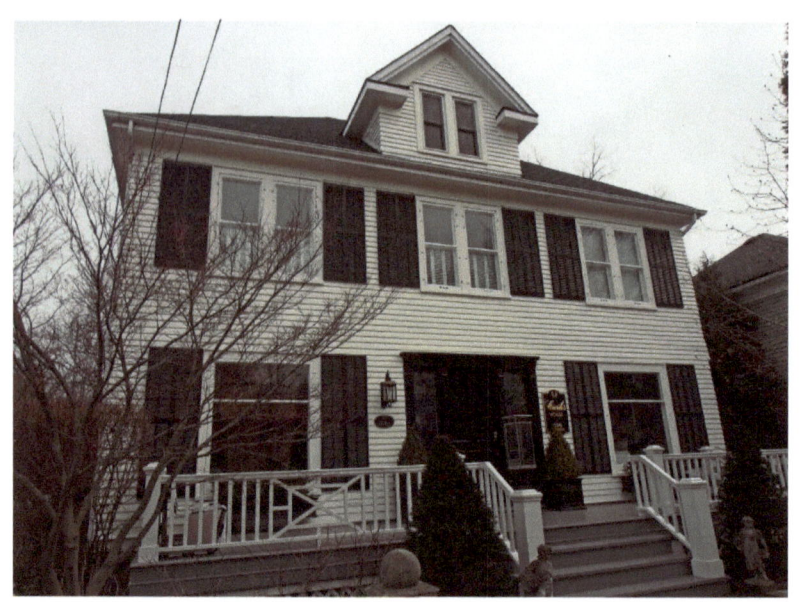

156 Gate Street – Ceciles House c. 1890 – Italianate, Cornice return on dormer gable

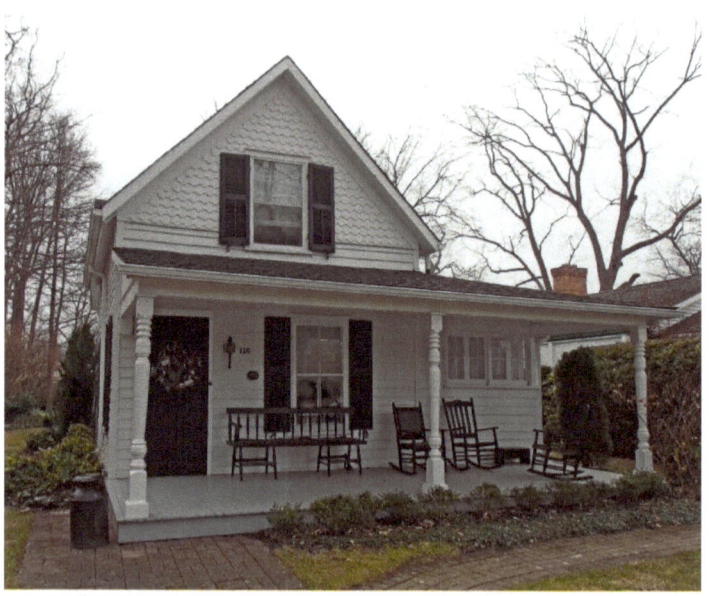

126 Gate Street – c. 1855 – Gothic Revival

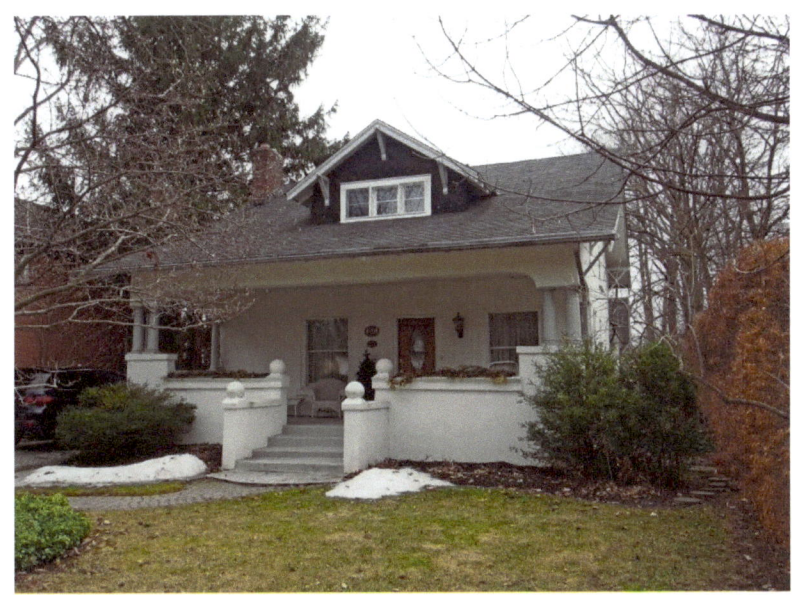

120 Gate Street - dormer

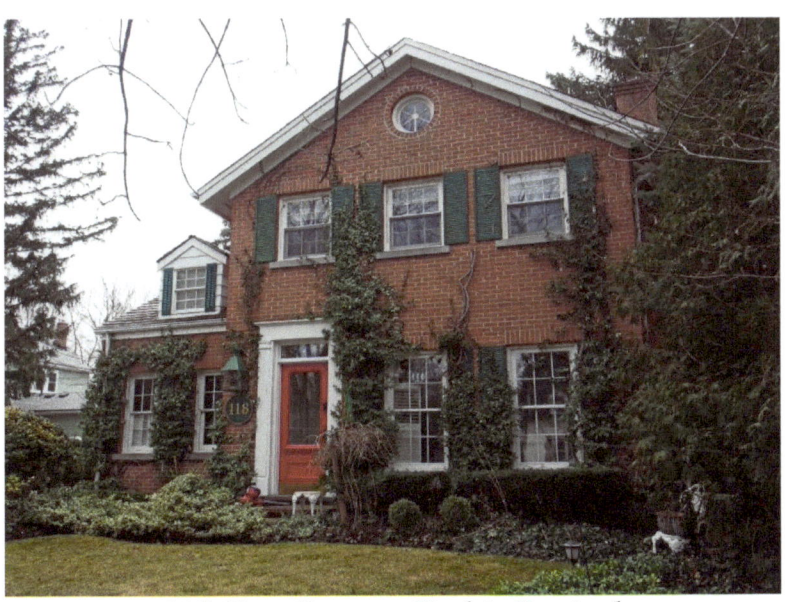

118 Gate Street – Gothic Revival

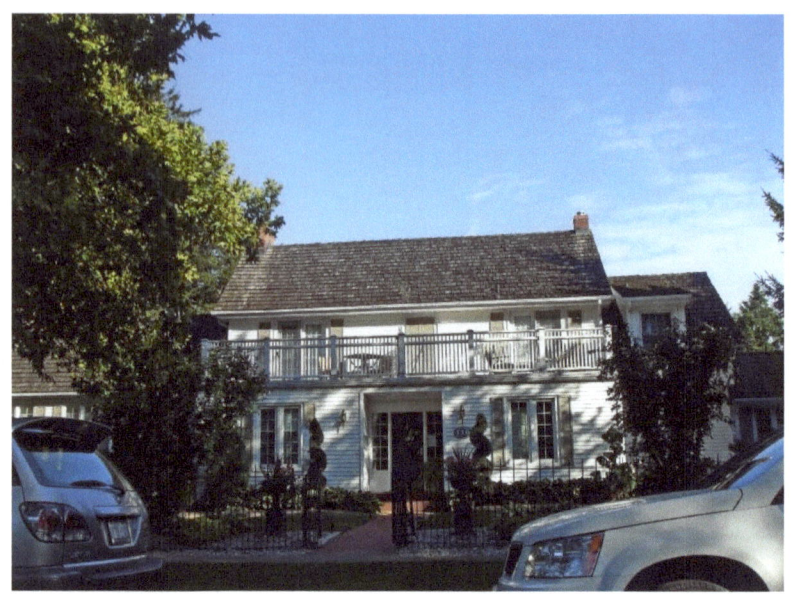

116 Gate Street – Greenview Bed & Breakfast

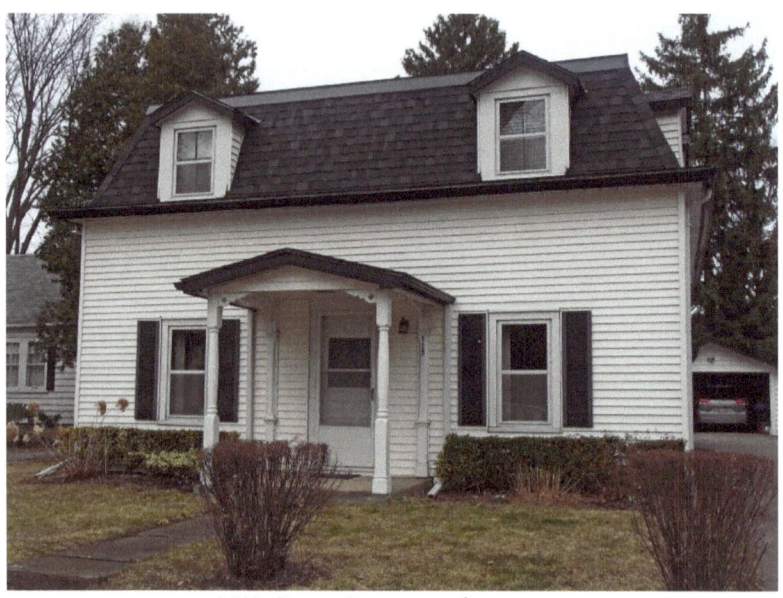

115 Gate Street - dormers

Architectural Terms

Brackets: a decorative or weight-bearing structural element which forms a right angle with one side against a wall and the other under a projecting surface such as an eave or roof. Example: 43 Castlereagh Street	
Buttress: a masonry structure built against or projecting from a wall which serves to support or reinforce the wall. In Canadian architecture, they are sometimes used for decoration. Example: Victoria Street, Grace United Church	
Cornice Return: decorative element on the end of a gable. Example: 233 King Street	
Cupola: A domed or curved roof rising from a building as a decorative element. Example: 43 Castlereagh Street	
Dentil Moulding: an even series of rectangles used as ornamental decoration in cornices. Example: Victoria Street, Grace United Church	
Dormer: (French for "sleep") a gable end window that pierces through the plane of a sloping roof surface to create usable space in the top floor or attic of a building by adding headroom. Example: Victoria Street	

Gable: the triangular portion of a wall between the edges of a sloping roof. Example: 463 King Street	
Hipped Roof: a roof where all sides slope downwards to the walls with no gables. Example: 225 King Street	
Keystones and Voussoirs: a voussoir is a wedge-shaped element used in building an arch. A keystone is the central stone that locks all the stones into position, allowing the arch to bear weight. A keystone is often enlarged and embellished. Example: 43 Castlereagh Street	
Mansard Roof: This style was popularized by Francois Mansart (1598-1666), an accomplished architect of the French Baroque period and especially fashionable during the Second French Empire (1852-1870). This roof is almost flat on the top section, with two slopes on each of its sides with the lower slope at a steeper angle than the upper and having dormer windows. Example: 236 King Street	
Pediment: a triangular section above the horizontal structure (entablature), typically supported by columns. The inside of the triangle is called the tympanum. Example: 287 Davy Street, see Page 23	
Pilaster: a slightly projecting column built into or applied to the face of a wall for additional structural support. Example: The Rogers-Blake-Harrison House	

Transom Window: the light above the doorway, also called a fanlight. Example: 43 Castlereagh Street	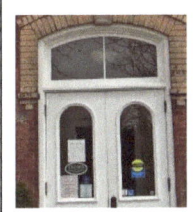
Turret: a small tower that projects from the wall of a building. Example: Regent Street, see Page 39	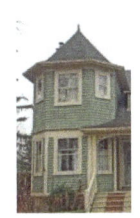
Vergeboard and Finial: also called bargeboards – hang from the projecting end of a roof and are often elaborately carved and ornamented. **Finial:** ornament added to the top of a gable, pinnacle, canopy or spire – a Gothic element. Example: finial - 43 Castlereagh Street Verge board: 125 Centre Street, see Page 43	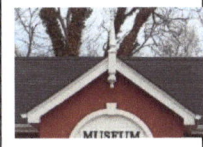

Building Styles

Georgian, before 1860 – This style began with the British King Georges in the 18th century. These buildings have balanced facades around a central door, medium-pitched gable roofs, and small paned windows. Example: 58 Johnson Street	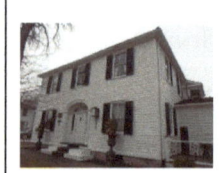
Gothic Revival, 1830-1890 – These decorative buildings have sharply-pitched gables with highly detailed vergeboards, pointed-arch window openings, and dichromatic brickwork. It is a common style in Ontario. Example: 463 King Street, see Page 19	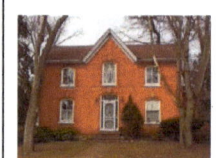
Italianate, 1850-1900 – It has wide-bracketed eaves, belvederes, wrap-around verandahs. Example: 277 King Street, see Page 16	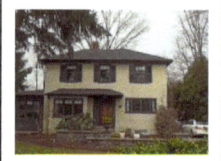
Queen Anne, 1885-1900 – This style is distinguished by an irregular outline featuring a combination of an offset tower, broad gables, projecting two-storey bays, verandahs, multi-sloped roofs, and tall, decorative chimneys. A mixture of brick and wood is common. Windows often have one large single-paned bottom sash and small panes in the upper sash. Example: 177 King Street, see Page 8	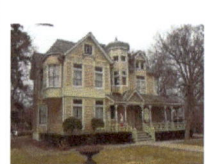

Saltbox: A saltbox is a building with a long, pitched roof that slopes down to the back, generally a wooden frame house. A saltbox has just one storey in the back and two stories in the front. The asymmetry of the unequal sides and the long, low rear roof line are the most distinctive features of a saltbox, which takes its name from its resemblance to a wooden lidded box in which salt was once kept. The earliest saltbox houses were created when a lean-to addition was added onto the rear of the original house extending the roof line sometimes to less than six feet from ground level. Example: 223 Johnson Street, see Page 37	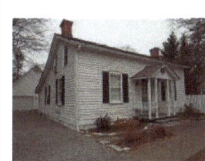
Second Empire, 1860-1880 – The mansard roof is the most noteworthy feature of this style and is evidence of the French origins. Projecting central towers and one or two-storey bays can also be present. Example: 236 King Street, see Page 11	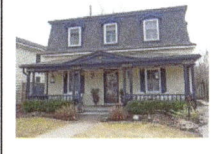

www.ingramcontent.com/pod-product-compliance
Lightning Source LLC
Chambersburg PA
CBHW040812200526
45159CB00022B/484